HOMES FOR A CHANGING CLIMATE

HOMES FOR A
CHANGING CLIMATE

ADAPTING OUR HOMES AND COMMUNITIES TO COPE
WITH THE CLIMATE OF THE 21ST CENTURY

WILL ANDERSON

green books

First published in 2009 by

GREEN BOOKS
Foxhole, Dartington
Totnes, Devon TQ9 6EB
www.greenbooks.co.uk

Design & layout
Stephen Prior

Printed in the UK by Latimer Trend.
Text printed on Emerald FSC paper
(75% recycled, 25% Forest Stewardship
Council approved).

Cover image:
New apartments on the Giudecca in
Venice. Photograph by Will Anderson.

ISBN 978 1 900322 47 8

Acknowledgements

My wholehearted thanks to all the people who informed, advised, supported and enabled the creation of this book.

Many people opened doors to their homes, lives and ideas. Thanks to Katerina Alifragi, Piers Allison, Justin Bere, Colin and Marie Carr, Rhoda and Neil Campbell, Maggie Fyffe, Lotte Glob, Bonnie Hewson, Christine and Pete Hope, Chris and Iain Learmouth, Ru Litherland, Nigel Lowthrop, Flora MacDonald, Martin Mackie, David Matzdorf, Janine Michael and Andy Moore, Russell Smith, Simon Tilley, Jo Woollcott, Nicholas and Heather Worsley, Tony Wrench, the residents of the Cotman Housing Association and the citizens of Seville. Thanks also to the Arnol Blackhouse Museum, the Beth Chatto Garden, Food Up Front, the Hockerton Housing Project and the Isle of Eigg Heritage Trust.

I am indebted to the following for their professional advice and insight: Gordon Anderson (Anderson Associates Ltd), Mary Arnold-Forster (Dualchas Building Design), Duncan Baker Brown (BBM Sustainable Design Ltd), Justin Bere (Bere Architects), Cor Beekmans and Arnoud de Bruijne (Nederlands Rijkswaterstaat), Stuart Bagshaw (Stuart Bagshaw & Associates), John Booth (Eigg Electric), Roger Budgeon (The Green Shop), Kiran Curtis (Kiran Curtis Associates), Nick Grant (Elemental Solutions), Francesca de Pol (Consorzio Venezia Nuova), Kerry Rankine and Julie Brown (Growing Communities), Andy Simmonds (Simmonds Mills Architects), Russell Smith (Parity Projects), Peter Smithdale (Constructive Individuals), Wayne Tatlow (Cotman Housing Association), Neil Winder (Studio MGM) and the members of the AECB.

For their interest, enthusiasm and support, thanks to Anne Anderson, Hari Beaumont, Sophie Branscombe, Karin Burnett, Robbie Currie, Sara Maitland, Margery Povall, Jane Powell, Norma Watson and especially Ford Hickson. The idea for the book was seeded by my late uncle, Allan Herriot.

I could not ask for a more supportive publisher. For their dedication, patience and hard work, thanks to Stephen Prior, Alethea Doran, Amanda Cuthbert, John Elford, Laura Myers, Bee West and Jon Clift.

The book would not have been possible without the work of the Met Office and the UK Climate Impacts Programme.

Photography credits

All photos by Will Anderson except the following.

Dave Maggs and David Barnes (page 62)
Kiran Curtis Associates (images pages 68 and 69)
The Green Shop (page 89 centre)
Consorzio Venezia Nuova (page 99 bottom right and image page 104)
Norfolk County Council library and information service (page 107 bottom right)
Andrew Lee (page 123 top and bottom left, page 125 top right, pages 164-5 and page 169)
Dualchas Building Design (page 125 top left)
Lucy Clarke (page 139)
Russell Smith (page 141)
Simmonds Mills Architects (page 142 top)
Thermal Inspections Ltd (page 142 bottom)

Contents

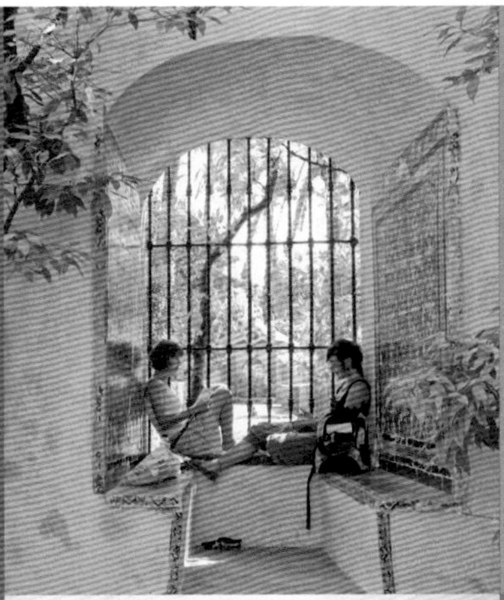

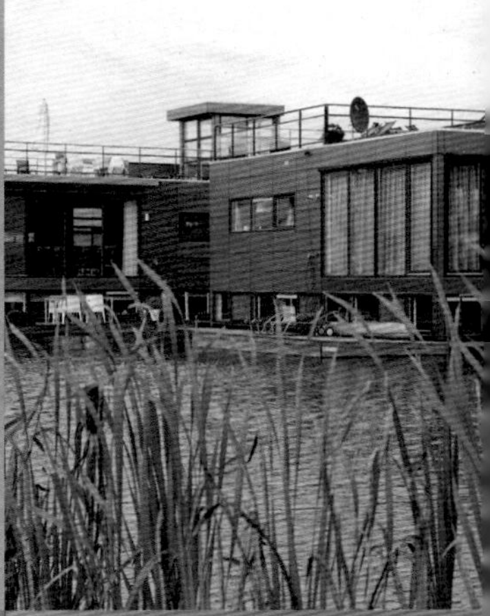

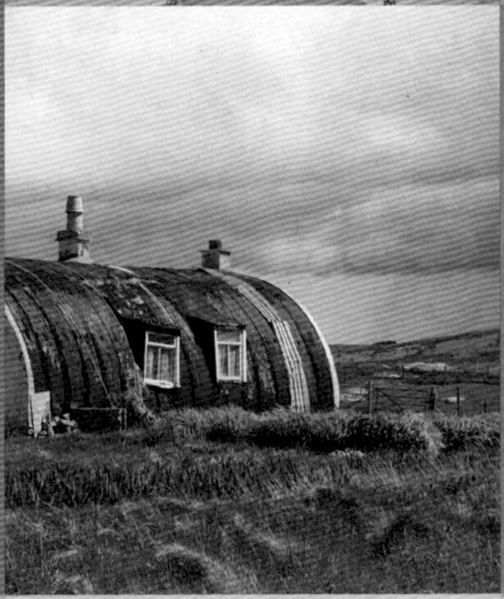

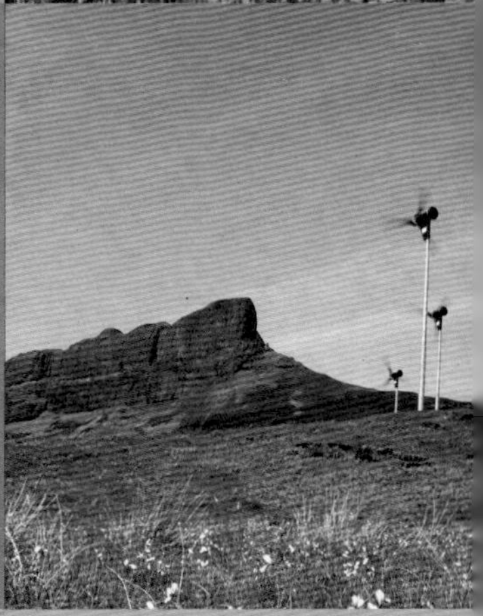

Introduction

Climate change is upon us. In Britain the effects are still relatively modest and can be hard to discern above the natural variability of the weather. But in recent years variations have been so pronounced – flooding, heatwaves and drought – that there seems little prospect of a happy return to the predictably unpredictable British climate. Furthermore, we know from the scientific evidence that global temperatures will continue to rise for the next 50 years even if the most optimistic predictions of future greenhouse gas emissions are achieved.[1] Our climate will take time to change but change is inescapable.

The fact that we cannot stop climate change does not mean that we should lessen our efforts to reduce emissions and create a low-carbon world. Today, people are dying from the effects of climate change, largely in vulnerable countries that do not have the resources for defence and adaptation.[2] Hence the challenge is no longer to stop climate change but to contain it and minimise its harm. The more we cut emissions, the less the world will suffer.

As the climate changes, we must change with it. We must learn to cope with heatwaves and floods; with storms and drought. We must make difficult decisions as sea levels rise – stay and defend, or retreat and relocate. At the same time, we will face the consequences of resource depletion, especially of the 'black gold' that fuels the modern world. Add to these problems the ever-rising global population and we find ourselves confronting the Gordian knot of food insecurity. What will happen to global food supplies when oil is scarce, the land increasingly desiccated and the weather full of tricks? We will face all of these problems in this century and, for better or worse, we must cope. If we want to cope for the better, we need to use our extraordinary gifts as human beings to imagine and prepare for the future, rethinking and redesigning almost everything.

The primary focus of this book is the built environment and houses in particular. Most of the houses we build, renovate or adapt today will still be with us in 10, 40 or 80 years' time. So we cannot put off building for the future. We are building for it now.

The fundamental message of the book is simple: we have been here before; we know what to do. We need not recoil from the threats that confront us, for we have tackled them a thousand times. Across the world, the great variety of human habitation demonstrates what we are capable of. Every extreme that Britain faces is already a reality somewhere in the world or somewhere in our own history. Adapting to climate change will be tough but we will survive. We will survive and thrive if, rather than continuing to exploit our depleted natural resources, we turn to our inexhaustible human resources instead: above all our adaptability and imagination.

Chapter one
The future unfolds

Georgian Bath: any dwelling is, first and foremost, an expression of culture and values.

Climate-adapted design

Every dwelling is the product of a curious inter-action between culture, geography and meteor-ology. Of these, culture is the dominant force. Our homes express our wealth and status, our hopes and aspirations, our social relations, our ideas of beauty, and our attitudes to the past and future. We fashion our homes in our own image, turning unpromising rooms and crumbling plaster into spaces layered by the memories, obsessions and minutiae of our everyday lives. We read the ideals of others in their choices of where and how they live.

These substantial forces find expression in materials that, in traditional buildings, reflect the geology and natural resources of the locality. Across Britain, the remarkable variety of buildings that people call home is testament to the riches of these resources: stone, clay and cob; timber, reed and straw. Vernacular buildings are as much rooted in geography, in the landscape itself, as in history, for the traditions of local building that define them have evolved through centuries of learning to make the best of local materials.

Underneath these layers of culture and geography, a dwelling offers one promise above all others: shelter from the storm. This is the singular function that all dwellings share, throughout the world. The challenges of climate may be radically different across the planet but the goal is always

The clay tiles and bricks of this traditional home locate it firmly in the south-east of England.

the same: a dry, still space at a comfortable temperature where we can rest, eat and hear each other speak. At every latitude, and at every contour line, buildings transform often harsh exterior conditions into comfortable indoor environments, often through nothing more than careful design and appropriate use of materials.

In modern times, cheap and plentiful energy has offered an easy solution to this task of climate adaptation. If it is possible to heat or cool a building by burning fossil fuels, we can design any which way in the knowledge that energy is always available to deliver indoor comfort. This freedom from the constraints of climate has transformed domestic architecture, although certain aspects of

building performance can only be addressed through design: the most radical and famous house of the twentieth century, Le Corbusier's Villa Savoye in Poissy, France, was hated by its owner, Mme Savoye, because the roof leaked.

The most robust climate-adapted buildings in the world tend to be in places where the climate is severe, for in extreme conditions there is no escaping the importance of good design. In contrast, most of Britain enjoys a relatively mild, temperate climate. As a result, British designers and builders have rarely shown much interest in creating homes that are well-adapted to climatic extremes. The people of Britain are used to living in homes that are cold and draughty in winter, provide little protection from heatwaves, and fall apart all too easily when a gale blows.

In recent years, this design laziness has been challenged by architects who have sought to design and build homes that are robust in winter conditions – homes that keep the cold out by design instead of compensating for penetrating cold with high-powered heating systems. Such homes stay comfortable and warm but have exceptionally low heating costs. The design of such homes is more complex than the design of ordinary high-energy homes but it is not rocket science: it requires only that architects pay close attention to their core concern – adaptation to climate.

If a dwelling can stay warm in the depths of winter with little or no energy input, can it also cope in a 35°C heatwave without air-conditioning, in a flood without sandbags, and in a windstorm without a visit from the loss adjuster? The answer is surely yes – it ought to be possible to design a house to cope with extremes such as these. Yet we do not do so as a matter of course for it is hard, when juggling the competing demands of a design specification, to push adaptation for seemingly unlikely events to the top of the list.

But what if we suspect that extreme events will cease to be so rare? What if we suspect that, in 30 years' time, the inhabitants of houses built today will no longer be enjoying the same gentle,

Somewhere in a forest in England. The simplest of dwellings may be little more than a roof and four walls, yet can still be an expression of humanity and beauty.

Cold winters are familiar in Britain but few of our homes are designed to cope with them. Even the grandest homes often have thin walls and draughty windows.

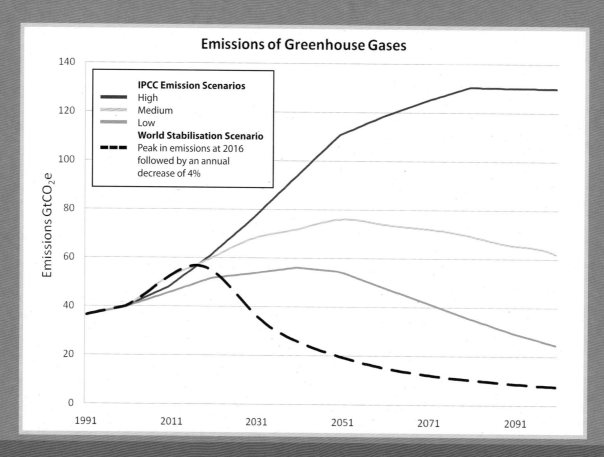

Emissions of Greenhouse Gases

IPCC Emission Scenarios
High
Medium
Low
World Stabilisation Scenario
Peak in emissions at 2016 followed by an annual decrease of 4%

Emissions $GtCO_2e$

(y-axis: 0, 20, 40, 60, 80, 100, 120, 140)
(x-axis: 1991, 2011, 2031, 2051, 2071, 2091)

Figure 1.1. Projections for global emissions of greenhouse gases, as defined by the scenarios of the Intergovernmental Panel on Climate Change.[2] © Defra 2009.

temperate climate that the people of Britain find endlessly fascinating but never very exciting? What if, in 60 years' time, the climate of Britain is unrecognisable?

In June 2009 the Met Office produced a new set of climate projections for the UK for every decade from the 2020s to the 2080s.[1] These projections describe changes in a wide range of climatic variables, including average and peak temperatures, the volume and intensity of rainfall, and humidity and cloud cover. They also include estimates for the extent of sea-level rise around the British coast. The projections were the product of a series of sophisticated climate models that capture the multiple chemical, biological and physical processes in the planet's atmosphere, oceans and land. Although there are significant variations in impacts across Britain, the overall pattern is clear: a hotter future

with drier summers, wetter winters and ever-rising sea levels. The intensity of both the heat and the rain will increase – there will be more heatwaves and downpours – but changes to storms and wind speeds have proved harder to predict.

The scale of these changes over the course of the century will depend on how successful we are in reducing the greenhouse gas emissions that are driving the process of climate change. The more carbon dioxide, methane and nitrous oxide we emit over the course of this century, the greater the changes in climate will be. To account for this, the Met Office climate projections describe the effects of three possible futures: low-, medium- and high-emissions scenarios. These scenarios, developed by the Intergovernmental Panel on Climate Change, are illustrated in Figure 1.1. Their impact on global mean temperatures is shown in Figure 1.2. Currently

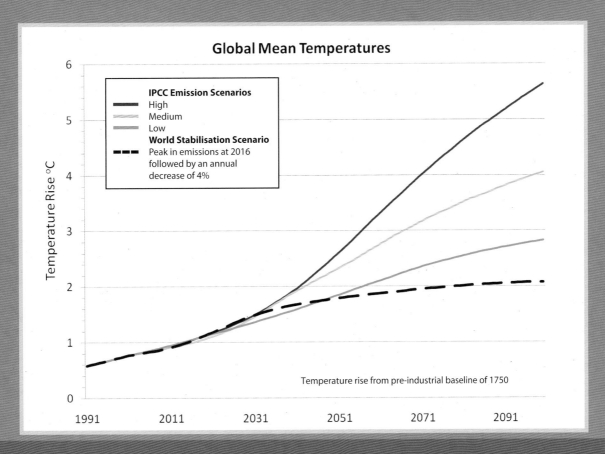

Figure 1.2. Projections for increases in global mean temperature, based on the emissions scenarios of the Intergovernmental Panel on Climate Change.[2] © Defra 2009.

we are on a pathway to medium or high emissions, for national and international efforts to reduce greenhouse gas emissions are still in their infancy. A genuinely international consensus on the threat of climate change was achieved only in 2008, with the election of US President Obama. If this consensus holds, a low-emissions future is possible.

There are, inevitably, other uncertainties involved in climate modelling. In particular, there is substantial natural variability in the Earth's climate which can affect weather patterns not only on a daily basis (through the movements of weather systems and storms) but also over years or even decades. If a sustained natural variation in the climate acts in the same direction as man-made climate change then the overall change will be that much bigger; if it acts in the opposite direction, the overall change will be that much smaller. The climate can also be affected by natural forces outside the climate system itself, such as changes in solar radiation and volcanic eruptions.

Beyond these natural sources of uncertainty, there are uncertainties in the climate models themselves, reflecting the fundamental difficulty of modelling a system as complex as the world's climate. Although climate models are all built on the best available scientific evidence, judgements have to be made about what this evidence implies. Assessments of the effects of feedback loops, such as changes in cloud cover that could either reflect more light away from the Earth or keep more heat in, are particularly diverse. Consequently, different climate models produce different results.

These problems are acknowledged in the 2009 projections. For every climate variable, every decade, and every emissions scenario, the Met Office describes a range of possible outcomes that reflects the range of uncertainty in the models. This makes it possible to differentiate between the middle of this range, which reflects the best fit of current evidence, and the extremes of the range, which are less likely but may be more serious. The maps reproduced in this book illustrate outcomes that are relatively unlikely (i.e. there is only a 10 per cent chance that the changes described will be more extreme) but have the most serious impacts. This is because buildings constructed today ought to be able to cope with all the possibilities that the century ahead may bring.

Even these probabilistic projections have their limitations: they can take account of 'known unknowns' but can say nothing of 'unknown unknowns'. However, as climate models have proved to be accurate in describing past changes in climate, it is unlikely that any unknown processes will change the projections fundamentally, at least for the next few decades. For all their uncertainties, the 2009 projections offer our best view yet of the unfolding climate of the twenty-first century.

The uncertainties inherent in the Met Office projections provide ample excuse for designers and builders to ignore the issue and carry on as usual. This is a familiar story: the uncertainties in the evidence for human-induced climate change kept ecological building on the margins until the case for change was overwhelming, by which time millions more high-energy houses had already been built. If we are to avoid a similar outcome – a generation of new houses built with no regard for the conditions of the near future – we need to start designing for these conditions now. As every architect knows, a constraint is always an opportunity for creativity. The case studies in the rest of this book demonstrate exactly this: robust, climate-adapted houses can be beautiful and desirable places to live.

If we want our homes to be comfortable and safe in the changing climate of the twenty-first century, our settlements and cities as well as our individual dwellings will have to adapt. For the external environment that a building seeks to shut out, or at least modulate into a habitable indoor environment, is itself a microclimate, affected by neighbouring buildings, surface materials, trees, vegetation and the lie of the land. Changes to these immediate conditions can have a profound effect on temperature and humidity and on exposure to wind, rain and surface rainwater. Our collective efforts to manage the environment immediately beyond our homes, including our gardens, will be as important in coping with the effects of climate change as the changes we make to our homes themselves.

The man-made environment in which any dwelling sits also includes an infrastructure for controlling the forces of nature, especially the rain, the rivers and the sea. Although there is scope for making individual dwellings more robust in the face of rising water levels, here the adaptation challenge is principally one that communities, of all sizes, must address.

For every climate impact, there is always a balance between what households can do to prepare for the future and what communities can do. Sometimes action is needed at a neighbourhood level; sometimes at a regional or even national level. Inevitably, decisions about who should do what will not always be straightforward. The challenge, however, is not only to find the optimal solutions across these arenas of action but also to ensure that these solutions bring benefits far beyond protection from the climate. Given our ability to transform the 'roof over our heads' into places of beauty and inspiration, we should expect no less for the transformation of our communities, towns and cities.

An ancient river flows between the back gardens of London terraces. The design of our settlements will be as important as the design of our dwellings in coping with the effects of climate change.

Chapter two
Heatwaves

Climate change projections for the UK

In the cool and rainy lands of northern Europe, heatwaves are still something of a rarity. As a result, the citizens of northern Europe are not always prepared when they occur. Although a prolonged period of settled, warm weather is still considered a treat by most of the British population, the consequences of severe heat can be serious: in 2003, over 2,000 people died in Britain due to the effects of the summer heatwave,[1] and many more died in scorching central France.

In other parts of the world, already stressed by high temperatures, the effects of ever-hotter conditions on lives and livelihoods will be potentially catastrophic. In Britain, higher temperatures will bring a mixture of benefits and unfamiliar problems. Having spent years working out how to keep the cold out of our homes, we will increasingly be faced with the problem of keeping our homes cool. It is vital that we achieve this without recourse to the energy-intensive option of air-conditioning. It will be ironic, tragic even, if our response to the effects of climate change is to find yet another way of adding greenhouse gases to the atmosphere.

Figure 2.1 shows the Met Office's 2009 projections of the increases in average summer temperatures by 2040 (from the 1961-1990 average) under three scenarios for future global greenhouse gas emissions – low, medium and high emissions. As historic emissions are the principal driver of change up to this date, there is relatively little difference between the scenarios. Figure 2.2 shows the projected increases by 2080. By this date, the effects of our possible future emissions are more pronounced.

The maps illustrate the upper end of the range of temperature projections, i.e. it is unlikely (only a 10 per cent chance) that temperatures will be higher than those illustrated, but they may well be lower. The upper end of the temperature projections is shown because any house built today ought to be robust enough to cope with this future: an increase of 5°C by 2040 and 9°C by 2080 in the south of England, under a high-emissions scenario. The rest of the country is not much cooler, with typical rises of 4°C by 2040 and 8°C by 2080. Even under a low-emissions scenario, average summer temperatures rise by 4°C by 2040 and 5-6°C by 2080.

The impact of these rising temperatures on maximum daily temperatures in the summer is shown in Figures 2.3 and 2.4, overleaf. Again, the upper end of the projected range of temperatures is shown: by 2040, 27°C could be common in the south under a high-emissions scenario; by 2080, 33°C would be the average daily top temperature in the summer. Further north, daily maximum temperatures in 2080 stay below 30°C even under a high-emissions scenario, and under low- and medium-emissions scenarios, average top temperatures do not exceed 30°C anywhere in Britain. These figures are, however, still averages, albeit averages of maximum daily temperatures. The Met Office projections also include the increase in the temperature of the hottest day of summer. The upper range of this increase, for a high-emissions scenario, is 8°C by 2040 and 14°C by 2080, throughout Britain.

Changes in the minimum night-time temperature are also important, because cool nights are vital in tempering hot days during heatwaves. In the south, night-time temperatures could rise, on average, to as high as 18°C in 2040 and 21°C in 2080 (the upper end of the projections under a high-emissions scenario). Although 21°C feels warm to those used to temperate English weather, it is still pleasantly cool after a day when the thermometer rises to 33°C.

In Europe, we can be confident that the twenty-first century will be a great deal warmer than the twentieth. This is true even though the Atlantic meridional overturning circulation (AMOC), commonly known as the Gulf Stream, is likely to slow down over this century. This slowdown has been incorporated into the climate models that define the temperature increases described in Figures 2.1 to 2.4. Although there is a risk that the AMOC could shut down altogether, this is currently considered to be highly unlikely.[2] The future is inescapably hot.

Low-emissions scenario

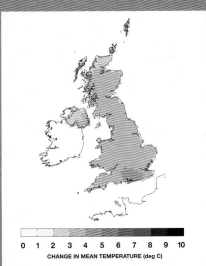

Data Source: Probabilistic Land
Future Climate Change: True
Variables: temp_dmean_tmean_abs
Emissions Scenario: Low
Time Period: 2030-2059
Temporal Average: JJA
Spatial Average: Grid Box 25Km
Location: -10.00, 48.00, 4.00, 61.00
Percentiles: 90.0
Probability Data Type: cdf2

Medium-emissions scenario

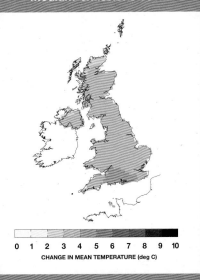

Data Source: Probabilistic Land
Future Climate Change: True
Variables: temp_dmean_tmean_abs
Emissions Scenario: Medium
Time Period: 2030-2059
Temporal Average: JJA
Spatial Average: Grid Box 25Km
Location: -10.00, 48.00, 4.00, 61.00
Percentiles: 90.0
Probability Data Type: cdf

High-emissions scenario

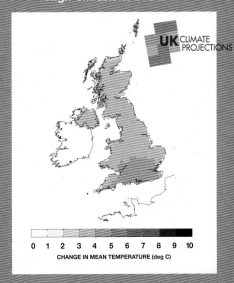

Data Source: Probabilistic Land
Future Climate Change: True
Variables: temp_dmean_tmean_abs
Emissions Scenario: High
Time Period: 2030-2059
Temporal Average: JJA
Spatial Average: Grid Box 25Km
Location: -10.00, 48.00, 4.00, 61.00
Percentiles: 90.0
Probability Data Type: cdf

Figure 2.1. The Met Office's 2009 projections of the increases in average summer temperatures by 2040 under three scenarios – low, medium and high greenhouse gas emissions. © UK Climate Projections 2009.

Low-emissions scenario

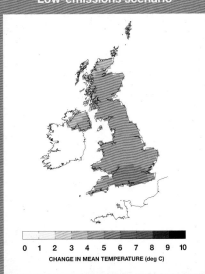

Data Source: Probabilistic Land
Future Climate Change: True
Variables: temp_dmean_tmean_abs
Emissions Scenario: Low
Time Period: 2070-2099
Temporal Average: JJA
Spatial Average: Grid Box 25Km
Location: -10.00, 48.00, 4.00, 61.00
Percentiles: 90.0
Probability Data Type: cdf

Medium-emissions scenario

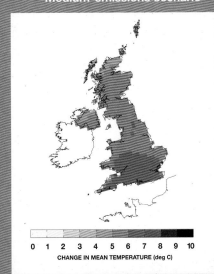

Data Source: Probabilistic Land
Future Climate Change: True
Variables: temp_dmean_tmean_abs
Emissions Scenario: Medium
Time Period: 2070-2099
Temporal Average: JJA
Spatial Average: Grid Box 25Km
Location: -10.00, 48.00, 4.00, 61.00
Percentiles: 90.0
Probability Data Type: cdf

High-emissions scenario

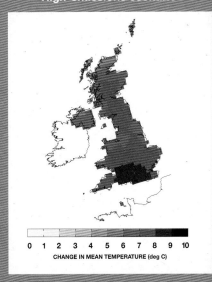

Data Source: Probabilistic Land
Future Climate Change: True
Variables: temp_dmean_tmean_abs
Emissions Scenario: High
Time Period: 2070-2099
Temporal Average: JJA
Spatial Average: Grid Box 25Km
Location: -10.00, 48.00, 4.00, 61.00
Percentiles: 90.0
Probability Data Type: cdf

Figure 2.2. The Met Office's 2009 projections of the increases in average summer temperatures by 2080 under three scenarios – low, medium and high greenhouse gas emissions. © UK Climate Projections 2009.

Low-emissions scenario

MAXIMUM TEMPERATURE (deg C)

Data Source: Probabilistic Land
Future Absolute Climate: True
Variables: temp_dmax_tmean_abs
Emissions Scenario: Low
Time Period: 2030-2059
Temporal Average: JJA
Spatial Average: Grid Box 25Km
Location: -10.00, 48.00, 4.00, 61.00
Percentiles: 90.0
Probability Data Type: cdf

Medium-emissions scenario

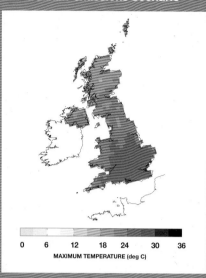

MAXIMUM TEMPERATURE (deg C)

Data Source: Probabilistic Land
Future Absolute Climate: True
Variables: temp_dmax_tmean_abs
Emissions Scenario: Medium
Time Period: 2030-2059
Temporal Average: JJA
Spatial Average: Grid Box 25Km
Location: -10.00, 48.00, 4.00, 61.00
Percentiles: 90.0
Probability Data Type: cdf

High-emissions scenario

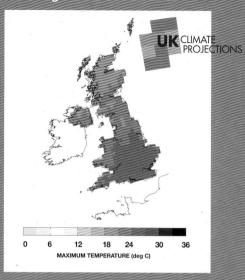

MAXIMUM TEMPERATURE (deg C)

Data Source: Probabilistic Land
Future Absolute Climate: True
Variables: temp_dmax_tmean_abs
Emissions Scenario: High
Time Period: 2030-2059
Temporal Average: JJA
Spatial Average: Grid Box 25Km
Location: -10.00, 48.00, 4.00, 61.00
Percentiles: 90.0
Probability Data Type: cdf

Figure 2.3. The Met Office's 2009 projections of the average daytime top temperatures in the summer months in 2040 under three scenarios – low, medium and high greenhouse gas emissions. © UK Climate Projections 2009.

Low-emissions scenario

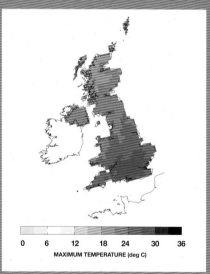

MAXIMUM TEMPERATURE (deg C)

Data Source: Probabilistic Land
Future Absolute Climate: True
Variables: temp_dmax_tmean_abs
Emissions Scenario: Low
Time Period: 2070-2099
Temporal Average: JJA
Spatial Average: Grid Box 25Km
Location: -10.00, 48.00, 4.00, 61.00
Percentiles: 90.0
Probability Data Type: cdf

Medium-emissions scenario

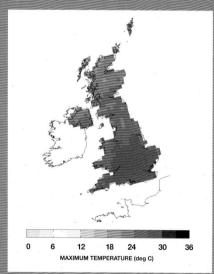

MAXIMUM TEMPERATURE (deg C)

Data Source: Probabilistic Land
Future Absolute Climate: True
Variables: temp_dmax_tmean_abs
Emissions Scenario: Medium
Time Period: 2070-2099
Temporal Average: JJA
Spatial Average: Grid Box 25Km
Location: -10.00, 48.00, 4.00, 61.00
Percentiles: 90.0
Probability Data Type: cdf

High-emissions scenario

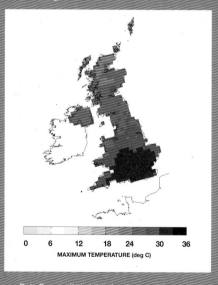

MAXIMUM TEMPERATURE (deg C)

Data Source: Probabilistic Land
Future Absolute Climate: True
Variables: temp_dmax_tmean_abs
Emissions Scenario: High
Time Period: 2070-2099
Temporal Average: JJA
Spatial Average: Grid Box 25Km
Location: -10.00, 48.00, 4.00, 61.00
Percentiles: 90.0
Probability Data Type: cdf

Figure 2.4. The Met Office's 2009 projections of the average daytime top temperatures in the summer months in 2080 under three scenarios – low, medium and high greenhouse gas emissions. © UK Climate Projections 2009.

The Passage de Valvanera, Seville, Spain.

Sheltering from the heat of the day: Seville, Andalucia

In the south of Spain the high peaks of the Sierra Nevada define the geological climax of a great arc of mountains that reaches from the Straits of Gibraltar to the east coast. To the south, the mountains descend to the reliably sunny beaches of the Costa del Sol, where European tourists gather in their hundreds of thousands. To the north, the mountains wrap around the low, fertile plain of the Guadalquivir river, where the heat in summer is more intense than almost anywhere else in Europe.

The ancient city of Seville lies at the heart of this plain. From the top of the Giralda, the bell-tower of the city's immense Gothic cathedral, the wide landscape appears to dissolve into a fine, flat haze. For most of the year the city enjoys a mild and agreeable climate, but in July and August the temperature regularly rises above 40°C in the shade. In the heat of the day the great yellow disc of the Seville bullring becomes a bright simulacrum of the fierce star overhead.

In the centre of old Seville the obvious place to seek shelter from the sun is the cathedral. The stone walls of the building are so thick that the heat cannot penetrate them, and the delicate windows are too occluded by stained glass to bring any significant warmth into the interior. Consequently both the inside air temperature and the surface temperatures of the floor and walls remain low throughout the day. However, although this provides an ideal environment for respite and prayer, a cathedral is an impractical design template for everyday living. Local lessons in heat-sensitive design are best sought not in the work of bishops but rather in the work of kings.

Across the square from the cathedral sits the Alcázar, the royal palace of Seville. It was built predominantly in the Mudéjar style, a fusion of Romanesque and Islamic design that flourished in the period following the defeat of the Moors and the return of Christian rule to southern Spain. Built in the fourteenth century for King Pedro of Castile, on the ruins of a Moorish fort, the Alcázar's form and details are manifestly indebted to the architects and craftsmen of the Islamic world to the east, a world where a blazing midday sun is a fact of life.

The bullring of Seville, still bright and hot under the late afternoon sun.

In the centre of the palace is the Patio de las Doncellas, the Courtyard of the Maidens. This exquisite interior–exterior space interprets a building form that is found across the Mediterranean and Middle East; its provenance the Roman atrium and 'peristyle' interior garden. The courtyard house flourished as a building form because it combines a well-lit habitable space with excellent temperature control. The Patio de las Doncellas illustrates all the techniques of climate-responsive design with immense style: differentiated living spaces, extensive shading, heavy materials, light surfaces, careful ventilation and abundant water and planting.

The courtyard is defined by the differentiation of three distinct spaces: the exposed centre, the transitional edge and the protected interior. Of these three spaces, the second offers a particularly attractive living environment in the heat of the day, awash with natural light but shaded from the direct sun. It is not difficult to imagine King Pedro's many courtiers and guests engaged in the business of the realm within these delicate galleries. The centre of the courtyard, exposed to the bright heat of the day, is occupied only by the garden and rill, with minimal access. The interior rooms of the palace lie behind the thick walls of the courtyard and have few openings. Protected by the transitional space of the gallery, they are restful spaces: darker, quieter and cooler.

Shading is the first and most effective line of defence against the sun, and here it is integral both to the overall form of the courtyard and to its many details. In the middle of the day, the extended eaves play a minor role compared with the galleries below them, which keep the direct sunlight off the interior walls. As the day progresses, the mutual shading provided by the opposing walls of the courtyard excludes the shallower rays of the sun. Individual windows also have shutters or curtains to banish all light if necessary.

Stone and ceramic finishes are used on all the floors and walls, keeping surface temperatures down. Our experience of heat in a building is affected as much by the heat radiated from the surfaces around us as

it is by the air temperature, so cooler surfaces are more comfortable in hot conditions. When you walk in to a stone building on a hot day, you immediately feel the effect of the cool radiation from the walls and floor regardless of the air temperature. The bright cream-white colours of the surfaces are also important in reflecting the sunlight and so reducing the amount of heat that the building absorbs. A dark wall exposed to the sun can have a surface temperature 10°C higher than a white wall in the same conditions.[3]

The interiors stay especially cool because they hold on to the cool of the night throughout the day. At night or in the early morning, the interiors

Gothic is not the only architectural style at play in the precincts of Seville's great cathedral.

The Patio de las Doncellas, the Courtyard of the Maidens, in the Alcázar palace.

are opened up and exposed to the cool air, shedding any heat that they have absorbed, then they are shut up again to keep direct light and warm air out during the day. This strategy is especially important in the upper apartments, the bedrooms, which must be kept cooler than the ordinary living quarters in order to ensure comfortable conditions for sleep. The courtyard itself holds on to a pool of cool night air, which the king, emerging from his bedroom for a late breakfast, would surely have appreciated.

Water and gardens have a special role in keeping buildings cool. In larger courtyards trees provide shade but here the emphasis is on water, which cools the environment both by absorbing heat – water is particularly good at this – and by evaporation, which also involves the extraction of a lot of energy from the surrounding air. The fountain that originally flowed at the centre of this courtyard would have assisted the process further. Plants of all sizes contribute to this evaporative effect as the transpiration of water from their leaves converts water into vapour. Water and greenery also play a psychological role in keeping heads cool in hard, bright surroundings. This is evident in the palace gardens, which bring together formal planting, water features, shady terraces and cool arbours. Even in the heat of the day it is possible to take a stroll around these gardens and feel refreshed.

So the King of Spain has a comfortable home (the upper apartments are still used by the royal family). But do these principles of passive cooling translate to everyday homes and living spaces? In fact they do, and rather well – in the old city of Seville there are hundreds of courtyard homes that adopt many, if not all, of the design ideas that informed the Patio de las Doncellas, albeit on a more modest scale.

The courtyards of Seville are private places, hidden behind the large and imposing doors that front the narrow streets. Moving from the hot and dusty streets through these heavy doors into the cool, interior courtyards is a delight, not least because there is such extraordinary variety in the design and decoration of the courtyards themselves. The smallest are effectively outdoor sitting rooms for single owners and are filled with personal effects. More often, the space is shared and a certain dignity is maintained, often with the careful placement of pot plants. The largest and grandest courtyards are lined with marble and include fountains and statues.

These domestic courtyards offer a cool, sheltered space, bathed in natural light but shaded from direct sunlight, where residents can sit outside at any time of day, protected from the heat of the sun and the noise and dust of the street. Sevillanos are sociable people and the courtyard provides a means of engaging with friends and neighbours at almost any time of day in comfortable conditions;

A terrace in the Alcázar buffers the cool interior from the direct heat of the sun.

The many and varied courtyards of the old city of Seville.

it is the city square in miniature.[4] If the temperature is too hot even here they can retreat into the interior rooms of the house, behind closed shutters. Every strategy of passive temperature control can be found within them: the cool, hard surfaces, usually finished in a light, reflective colour; the shading provided by galleries, rooftop blinds and the tall, narrow building form; and the evaporative cooling of plants and water features. Although the courtyards do not encourage ventilation in the heat of the day, they enable warm air from the surrounding apartments to be exhausted when the external air is cooler, and in the morning they retain cool wells of night air. Ventilation is an effective cooling strategy only if the outside air temperature is lower than the temperature inside. This is usually the case in northern Europe, at least at present, but in southern Europe ventilating a house during the hot period of the day is usually a bad idea as the warm air will make the building hotter still. This is why the people of Seville shut up their windows in the middle of the day but open them to the cool air of night or early morning.

Ventilation is useful not only for flushing warm air out of a building but also for its direct cooling effect. Human beings are very sensitive to the effect of air passing over their skin: a cool breeze on a hot day has a profound effect on our comfort, as does a cold draught on a winter's day. This form of summer cooling can easily be produced with a fan, electric or otherwise, but it is often possible to catch or channel natural air flows to achieve the same result. In Seville, the midday air in the summer streets is usually still and warm but there is a better chance of air movement at roof level. Consequently roof balconies are very popular; these are designed, decorated and planted with as much enthusiasm as the courtyards below.

The most basic form of heat protection, solar shading, is also subject to a striking variety of

Roof terraces catch the breeze when the air in the streets below is hot and still.

The Sevillanos use every method possible to protect the cool interiors of their homes, including shutters, blinds, curtains, vegetation, louvres, balconies and awnings.

VALPARAISO 36

interpretations on the streets of Seville. As window shading is principally used to prevent overheating, it is normally installed on the outside of windows, but may be combined with curtains or blinds on the inside in order that temperature, glare and privacy can all be controlled in different conditions. Some methods, such as roller shutters, are designed to seal the window entirely, keeping warm air as well as sunlight out. However, some degree of control over ventilation is usually possible. For example, heavy fabric blinds which cover the whole window can also be draped over the edge of a balcony railing in front of the window to allow some air and indirect light in.

In general, the more adaptable a shading system is the better, for not only are there different conditions to deal with across the day and the year but also different people have quite different opinions about what constitutes a comfortable temperature for everyday living.

Outside the old city walls of Seville, few houses follow the traditional courtyard design. The familiar forms of dense urban living are more in evidence: many and varied apartment blocks, both high- and low-rise. The linear apartment block may not be as sophisticated as the courtyard house, but a two-storey masonry block will

Multiple methods of shading and cooling are in evidence across the face of this tower block in the centre of Seville.

Left: The heat of the day is comprehensively shut out of this villa, which is cooled by climbing vegetation.

Right: Windows have always been important to modernist architects, but in the heat of Seville external roller blinds are a necessary addition.

perform well in the heat if it is set out on an east–west axis with well-shaded living spaces to the south and bedrooms to the north.[5] Although the ugly backsides of air-conditioning units are common in this harsher streetscape, passive cooling strategies still dominate. Across the face of a single tower block a multitude of shading methods is articulated, turning the order of mass-housing design into a playful pattern of solar defences.

At the other end of the economic scale, detached villas have the space and means to employ a wider range of passive cooling strategies. The two illustrated above both employ relatively small windows, light surfaces and heavy materials that hold on to the cool of the night and warm up slowly. The first has tightly fitting shutters to exclude the heat of the day and employs climbing plants on the walls to help cool the concrete. The second, designed by Josep Lluís Sert after a spell in the studio of le Corbusier, is a modernist gem, though the external roller blind on the primary window is definitely a local detail.

Beyond the design of individual dwellings and apartment blocks, the form of the city and the behaviour of its inhabitants also alleviate the excesses of the summer heat. In the narrow streets of the old city, the mutual shading of opposing buildings protects pedestrians from the direct sun. But if buildings are too densely packed they will overheat together and struggle to cool down. So the courtyards of the Alcázar are mimicked in the many squares and gardens of the city, which break up the hard, hot fabric of the built environment. The trees and vegetation in these squares and parks play a part in keeping the city cool, providing shade and cooling the air through their constant transpiration of the rainwater that soaks into the porous ground. Fountains perform a similar role, cooling the air and soaking eager passers-by.

Into these public spaces the people of Seville pour as the hot afternoon gives way to the sociably warm evening. In a single square an entire neighbourhood may gather, the children playing together while the adults drink, gossip and flirt, relishing the air and light after their enclosure during the day's hot high noon. It is a way of life that follows the temperature gradient across the day, a way of life that even air-conditioning is unlikely to render obsolete.

Keeping cool in the city: shade, vegetation, light clothes and ice cream.

the old city the introduction of air-conditioning makes it possible for the traditional cool materials of stone and ceramic tiles to give way to materials such as wood and plastic, which warm up almost as quickly as the air itself. Nonetheless Sevillanos are proud of the beauty of their historic city and it seems highly unlikely that their graceful court-yards, elaborate windows and secret roof terraces will be replaced any time soon by an army of hideous, growling air-conditioning systems.

A green and pleasant land

From the hot streets of Seville Britain seems distant and cold, lying far beyond the mountains that protect southern Europe from the north Atlantic storms and keep the African heat comfortably settled over the Mediterranean in the summer. In Britain's infamously changeable climate a hot summer day is still a gift, a fleeting pleasure to be enjoyed before the clouds and rain return. As soon as the temperature rises above 25°C the gardens and parks of the nation bloom with prostrate sun-worshippers, delighting in the warmth of the precious solar rays.

The back gardens and parks of British cities will prove to be invaluable assets as heatwaves become less exceptional and more the norm. Cities are particularly vulnerable to heatwaves because their excess of concrete, tarmac and brick creates significant temperature differences between the centre of the city and the surround-ing countryside, a phenomenon known as the 'urban heat island effect'. In London this temp-erature difference can be as much as 7°C.[6] As in Seville, adding vegetation and green space can make a big difference to this effect: the addition of 10 per cent green cover to a dense built-up area such as a town centre has the potential to reduce the temperature by 2-3°C.[7] The opportunity for reducing overheating through green urban design is therefore enormous.

Unquestionably, however, the advent of air-conditioning is changing the city. If you can achieve an ideal interior temperature by plugging a box into the wall, why go to the trouble of incorporating passive cooling measures into your house designs? Even in the courtyard houses of

Britain has a long tradition of integrating green spaces within cities. Public parks have always been a focus of civic pride and are now universally

Bedford Park, the model for a thousand leafy English suburbs.

Britain's first garden suburb, was set out by developer Jonathan Carr in the 1870s. Carr recognised the value of the mature trees in his west London plot and so planned his roads to wiggle around them. As a result, the estate felt as if it had grown organically like an old English village. Today the Queen Anne houses with their white picket fences still stand but many of the old trees have gone, replaced by small ornamentals such as birches, which are of little value in cooling the streetscape.

Bedford Park became an inspiration for the garden city movement, which took the integration of green space and urban form to a new level and defined the form of Welwyn and Letchworth Garden Cities in England and many other towns and suburbs across the world. Today the tradition lives on, a vital touchstone for architects and developers who understand that the spaces between houses are just as important as the spaces within them. The 'leafy suburbs' that follow this tradition will be invaluable in the hotter years to come.

Planning regulations today require that housing is built to a much higher density than at Bedford Park or any other Victorian suburb. Consequently there is more building fabric to cool and an even greater need for vegetation, even if the room for it is harder to find. The award-winning Accordia development in Cambridge demonstrates that this need not be a problem. The design was shaped by the idea of 'living in a garden', inspired in part by the beautiful courtyards and gardens of the colleges of the university. The rows of terraced housing are bordered by a deep-green line of mature trees. Between the terraces there are newly planted communal gardens. The houses themselves incorporate roof terraces, balconies and courtyard gardens where pot plants and climbers flourish. The overall effect is indeed of a richly planted English garden.

The most radical approach to greening the city landscape, and one of the most effective ways of bringing down urban temperatures,[8] is to cultivate roofs. Most modern 'green roofs' are not very deep and can support only drought-resistant plants

recognised to be a vital part of the urban landscape. However, to cool every corner of the urban environment this greenery must find its way up every street, turning the entire city into a garden. Happily the 'garden city' is a long-established ideal of British urban planning: Bedford Park,

'Living in a garden': the Accordia housing development in Cambridge.

such as sedums and sempervivums but, with the right engineering to support you, it is possible to create a fully fledged garden. As with ordinary gardens at ground level, such roof gardens have many functions, not only cooling the house and the street but also filtering pollutants out of the air, reducing the speed with which rainfall hits the drains and even supplying food.

To stay cool, cities of the twenty-first century need to combine the hard fabric of buildings, paving and concrete with a green infrastructure of parks, open spaces, woodlands, community gardens, water courses, allotments, private gardens, tree-lined streets, fields and green roofs. The revival of the garden city is long overdue, though perhaps the modern form should look for inspiration not only to Ebenezer Howard's quintessential English garden but also to woodlands, hedgerows, smallholdings and water meadows.

A modest tradition of keeping cool

The British love of parks and gardens is fortunate, as the prevention of overheating has rarely been a significant concern of the designers and builders of individual homes. Furthermore, the people who live inside these homes often have little idea of how to adjust or adapt their homes to alleviate the heat. When the temperature soars, most people respond individually and bodily, taking their clothes off, eating ice cream and drinking beer, but have no expectation that the buildings they live in could also play a role in keeping them cool. Conservatories are often added to living spaces without any consideration of how they will perform on sunny days, typically leading to rapid overheating and the hasty retrofitting of inadequate shading or air-conditioning.

This attractive house in North London is maintained by keen gardener and green-roof enthusiast David Matzdorf. The richly planted roof is even more effective than his well-planted garden in keeping the house cool.

The city as a fine weave of built form, water and vegetation.

In northern Europe, shading is mainly used to control glare and protect privacy rather than to prevent overheating. Curtains, blinds and shutters are typically hung on the inside of windows, where they have limited value in reducing overheating because once light has got through the glass it will turn into heat trapped within the room, regardless of what lies between the glass and the rest of the room. Light colours on the rear of curtains and blinds help to reflect the light straight back out of the window, but much of the light will be absorbed by the material and become heat.

This is not to say that all houses in Britain cope poorly with high temperatures. In fact many houses built with heavy masonry or stone walls stay cool thanks to the slow responses of these materials to changes in air temperature (they also take a long time to warm up in winter for the same reason). Many urban Victorian homes have substantial basements that are ideal retreats on hot days as they admit relatively little light and benefit from the steady, cool temperature of the ground. Victorian sash windows provide good ventilation if used properly: to maximise the flow of air through the window the sashes should be positioned so the window is open equally at the top and bottom. Separating the in-flow and out-flow enables cooler air entering through the bottom opening to flush warm air out of the top.[9]

There are also examples of developments in the modern era where good design makes a difference on hot days. One such development is the Barbican in the City of London. This estate is very much a product of the mid-twentieth century modernist mindset and includes massive concrete structures raised above public walkways, imposing towers and uniform, weather-stained finishes. In the hands of lesser architects (and poorer clients), these ingredients have spelled disaster elsewhere in Britain, but the quality of the design in the Barbican has passed the test of time. Although the Arts Centre in the middle of the estate is famously bodged and inaccessible, the housing that dominates the estate still expresses the muscular optimism of the modernist dream.

Most of the principles employed to cool the masonry-built old city of Seville can be seen at work in the grand concrete of the Barbican. In the centre of the estate the courtyard form is writ large, the blocks of flats looking out on to both a miniature forest glade, where residents can enjoy the deep shade of mature trees, and a formal watercourse that spills from a great funnel at one end of the site and flows sedately round sunken gardens, under one of the great residential blocks and through a broad canal where fountains play. This green-and-blue heart of the development complements the massed concrete of the buildings, which would otherwise be too harsh and hot for comfort. Concrete does, however, take time to heat up and so responds slowly to extreme daytime temperatures. This in turn requires that the nights are cooler: then the three great towers of the Barbican become cooling fins, shedding the sun's energy into the dark sky.

Every flat enjoys wide views through large windows, set back within their balconies so that the

The courtyard form writ large: the Barbican, London.

high summer sun cannot reach the interiors. This simple and effective design keeps direct light (and therefore heat) out but allows indirect light in. However, it is effective only for south-facing homes, for it offers little protection against the low sun of the late afternoon and evening. For the inhabitants of west-facing flats, it is back to basics with blinds and curtains in the battle against overheating.

The passively cooled home

My own home in South London, Tree House, was built at the beginning of the twenty-first century with an eye to the summer temperatures that might be common in the south-east of England by the end of the century. Everything was done to ensure that the house would stay cool passively, without recourse to air-conditioning, even in the hottest summers.

In Tree House, as in the old houses of Seville, the primary concern is to stop the heat getting in. Although the house has no south-facing windows, which always present the biggest overheating risk (in the northern hemisphere), there are very large windows on both the east and west facades. At the top of the house, the east-facing window of the study is set back from the roofline and protected from the high summer sun by deep eaves. The eponymous tree also provides excellent seasonal shading: its canopy protects the building in summer but admits the welcome warmth of the direct sunlight in the winter. At the back of the house, where the main living space opens west-ward, shading is provided by external aluminium venetian blinds and a framework of fixed wooden louvres (a *brise-soleil*, or sun-breaker).

Tree House is extremely well insulated. Although the primary purpose of this insulation is to keep the

Tree House is designed to stay cool passively. Techniques used include the shade from a deep roof overhang and deciduous tree at the front of the house (top left) and external venetian blinds and fixed louvres at the back (top right); 'passive stack' ventilation, which exhausts warm air through the roof windows at the top of the house, drawing cooler air into the bottom of the building (middle left); cool finishes, which are slow to heat up (middle right); water and fountains (bottom left); and a richly planted courtyard garden (bottom right). Architect: Constructive Individuals.

heat in during the cold winter months, the insulation in the roof (in particular) also plays an important role in keeping the heat out during summer heatwaves. Loft rooms under uninsulated roofs can become unbearable in summer as the roof radiates the heat it absorbs from the sun on to the sweating inhabitants below. The house also has a compact form so the total external wall and roof area is not too big compared with the volume of the house (a low surface-to-volume ratio). This helps to reduce the amount of heat that flows through the walls both outwards, in the winter, and inwards, during summer heatwaves. Most of the external surface is covered in a white render, which reflects the light and so reduces heat absorption.

The windows of Tree House can be opened to allow both cross-ventilation and bottom-to-top (passive stack) ventilation. The study at the top of the house is the most vulnerable to overheating, but windows can be opened on both the east and west walls, allowing the prevailing breeze to flow through and flush out any build-up of heat. The entire house can be cooled overnight by opening a secure window over a formal pond on the ground floor and a high window in the study. Cool air is drawn across the pond, which cools it further, and warm air is flushed out of the top of the house. By the morning the house is purged of heat and ready to cope with another boiling day.

Although the house is built principally of timber, a lightweight material that responds quickly to changes in temperature, small but important adjustments were made to the finishes in order to reduce the risk of rapid temperature swings and help to keep surface temperatures cool. All the walls are finished with two layers of plasterboard and the ground-floor living room is finished in slate. This room is protected from the sun until late in the day and so holds on to the cool of the night in the fabric of its finishes.

Finally, the small courtyard garden at the back of Tree House may not offer quite the same cooling potential as the interior courtyards of Seville, but the water and planting contribute to the well-being of the inhabitants thanks not only to the cooling effects of evaporation and transpiration but also to the psychological effect of living every day within a flourishing garden.

What you can do

If you want to stay comfortable in your home during a heatwave without hiring an energy-hungry air-conditioner, focus on shading, ventilation and the use of cool, heavy materials. Shading is the number-one priority: a shaded house will stay cooler than a house with windows exposed to the sun. Ventilation will help keep your home cool as long as the outside air is cooler than the air inside. Materials such as stone, masonry, brick and tiles will help to maintain the cool interior of your home over a sustained heatwave as long as the materials are exposed to a minimum of direct sunlight during the day and, ideally, have the benefit of cool ventilation at night.[10]

If your home only occasionally overheats, try the following measures.

- Close curtains, blinds or shutters early in the day in the rooms that overheat. If you need some natural light in these rooms during the day, install adjustable blinds that block direct sunlight but admit indirect light.

- If possible, improvise external shading for windows exposed to direct sunlight.

- Keep windows closed as well as shaded in the heat of the day. When the outside air temperature is cooler, find the best way of opening windows to create cooling draughts through your home (leaving a gap at the bottom and top of a sash window is effective for a room that cannot be cross-ventilated).

- In a prolonged heatwave, open windows at night or first thing in the morning to flush out warm air and cool the building.

If your home regularly overheats, begin by identifying exactly where the problem lies. Which rooms are the most uncomfortable to be in? Which windows let in too much direct sunlight? Is there a problem at the top of your house, underneath a roof with no insulation? Does the whole house get hot and then stay hot at night?

In rooms that get hot because of direct sunlight, do the following in order of priority.

- Install external shading such as shutters, blinds, louvres, pergolas and awnings, and plant hedges and trees. These should be robust enough to cope with the weather and, where appropriate, adaptable to respond to different light needs across the day or year (shutters are very adaptable; fixed louvres are not). Remember that it is principally direct light that you are trying to block. Consider whether you need shading in summer from a high sun (south-facing windows) or a low sun (west-facing windows), and choose your shading method accordingly.

- Improve daytime and night-time ventilation (see previous page).

- Install hard, cool floors such as ceramic tiles, slate or other stone. If you are worried that this will be too cold in winter, use a rug when the summer is over.

- Install internal shading with a light, reflective finish on the window side. This is not as effective as external shading but will help to reflect the light back out of the window.

- Fill the rooms affected with house plants, especially plants that transpire rapidly, such as the peace lily (*Spathiphyllum wallisii*).

If your whole house gets hot, consider the following options as well.

- Find out how much insulation there is in the roof. If there is little or none, install some more. The recommended depth of loft insulation is 270mm. Cavity or external wall insulation will also help.

- Install low-energy lights and appliances, as all the electrical energy you use at home ends up turning into heat. If you have a hot water tank, make sure it is well insulated.

- Paint the outside of the house white.

- Plant up as much of your outside space as you can. Grow climbers up the walls. If you have an accessible flat or shallow-pitched roof, consider a green roof.

- If you are still tempted to install air-conditioning, try an evaporative cooler instead as they use less energy than an air-conditioning unit.

Conservatories are a special problem. They overheat in summer and freeze in winter, and are rarely a comfortable temperature.

- If you are adding a conservatory to a living space, keep the two rooms separate with a door between them. This will reduce heat losses through the conservatory in the winter and prevent the conservatory cooking the house during summer heatwaves.

- Install external shading wherever possible. A fixed wooden lattice over a conservatory roof provides an ideal supporting framework for a deciduous climber. You could train climbers over the vertical windows too.

- Internal blinds are also useful, though principally to reduce glare. Make sure they have bright, reflective outer surfaces.

- Stone floors and masonry or brick walls will help absorb the heat. Do not cover up the outer stone or brick wall of your house when it becomes the inner wall of your new conservatory.

- Make sure that roof and window vents are easily accessible and adjustable.

- Fill with lush and shady planting.

This striking development for Metropolitan Housing Trust by Anne Thorne Architects boasts exterior shutters and exceptionally deep eaves, both of which protect the interior of the building from direct sunlight.

Chapter three
Floods

Climate change projections for the UK

Floods can come from all directions. The most devastating floods are usually river floods: when a river bursts its banks the impact on neighbouring property and land is immediate and potentially catastrophic, especially if sewers also flood. However, periods of intense rainfall can also cause surface water flooding, or 'flash floods', which can happen almost anywhere but are common in built-up areas where the ground is impermeable and the capacity of the drains limited. Again, if stormwater drains are connected to sewers, the consequences can be dire. If, on the other hand, the geology of the ground beneath your feet is permeable, the water may come from below. Groundwater flooding can last for months. Finally, tidal flooding is a risk for Britain's many estuarine and coastal communities, especially when tides are driven high by storm surges.

The British population has a long tradition of messing about in boats and enjoying the pleasures of rivers, canals and the seaside. But in 2007 the romance of living with water was rudely challenged when cities, towns and villages across the country found themselves under water. Intense rainfall overwhelmed drains and pushed rivers beyond their bounds. On Friday 20th July up to five inches of rain fell in one day in the area surrounding the Gloucestershire town of Tewkesbury, which sits at the confluence of the Severn and Avon rivers. The rivers duly burst their banks and the residents of the town found themselves living on a soggy island, surrounded by flooded fields and roads.

The severity of the 2007 floods exposed the vulnerability of many British homes to intense and prolonged rainfall. The subsequent Pitt Review acknowledged that the risks of flooding are not only increasing, they are also changing. To the relatively well-understood risks of river and coastal flooding we must now add the much more unpredictable risk of flash floods. The review concluded:

"Flood risk is here to stay . . . the country should confront these mounting challenges and adapt accordingly, recognising that this process of adaptation will take place over a generation."[1]

The youngest generation of the twenty-first century does indeed have some damp winters to look forward to (despite the experience of recent years, summers are expected to get much drier). Figure 3.1 shows the Met Office's 2009 projections for increases in winter rainfall by 2040 (from the 1961-1990 average) under the three scenarios for future global greenhouse gas emissions. As historic emissions are the principal driver of change up to this date, there is relatively little difference between the scenarios in 2040. Figure 3.2 shows the projected increases to 2080. By this date, the effects of our possible future emissions are clear.

The maps illustrate the upper end of the range of rainfall projections, i.e. it is unlikely (only a 10 per cent chance) that rainfall will be higher, but it may well be lower. The upper end of the rainfall projections is shown because any house built today ought to be robust enough to cope with this future: increases in winter rainfall of between 20 and 40 per cent by 2040 and 70 per cent in many areas by 2080, under a high-emissions scenario. Even under a low-emissions scenario, increases in rainfall of up to 50 per cent are possible by 2080, and even higher in the far north-west of Scotland.

An increase in winter rainfall of even 20 per cent seriously increases the risk of winter flooding, especially as the intensity of the rain – the amount that falls in any rainstorm – is also likely to increase. Figures 3.3 and 3.4, overleaf, illustrate the projections for the increase in rainfall on the wettest day. Again, the upper end of the range of possibilities is shown: a 30 per cent increase in most areas by 2040 and 50-70 per cent increases common by 2080 under a high-emissions scenario. Even an increase in rainfall intensity of 30 per cent, as shown in many parts of Britain under a low-emissions scenario, would have serious consequences.

Low-emissions scenario

CHANGE IN PRECIPITATION (%)

Data Source: Probabilistic Land
Future Climate Change: True
Variables: precip_dmean_tmean_perc
Emissions Scenario: Low
Time Period: 2030-2059
Temporal Average: DJF
Spatial Average: Grid Box 25Km
Location: -10.00, 48.00, 4.00, 61.00
Percentiles: 90.0
Probability Data Type: cdf

Medium-emissions scenario

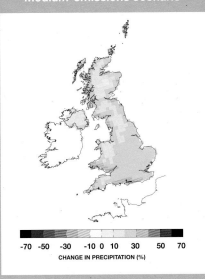

CHANGE IN PRECIPITATION (%)

Data Source: Probabilistic Land
Future Climate Change: True
Variables: precip_dmean_tmean_perc
Emissions Scenario: Medium
Time Period: 2030-2059
Temporal Average: DJF
Spatial Average: Grid Box 25Km
Location: -10.00, 48.00, 4.00, 61.00
Percentiles: 90.0
Probability Data Type: cdf

High-emissions scenario

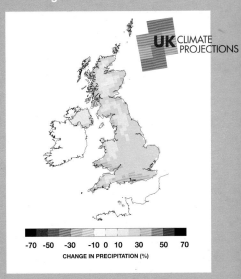

CHANGE IN PRECIPITATION (%)

Data Source: Probabilistic Land
Future Climate Change: True
Variables: precip_dmean_tmean_perc
Emissions Scenario: High
Time Period: 2030-2059
Temporal Average: DJF
Spatial Average: Grid Box 25Km
Location: -10.00, 48.00, 4.00, 61.00
Percentiles: 90.0
Probability Data Type: cdf

Figure 3.1. The Met Office's 2009 projections of the increases in winter rainfall by 2040 under three scenarios – low, medium and high greenhouse gas emissions. © UK Climate Projections 2009.

Low-emissions scenario

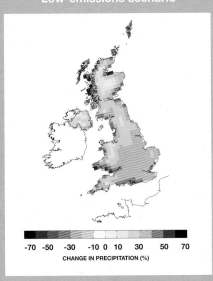

CHANGE IN PRECIPITATION (%)

Data Source: Probabilistic Land
Future Climate Change: True
Variables: precip_dmean_tmean_perc
Emissions Scenario: Low
Time Period: 2070-2099
Temporal Average: DJF
Spatial Average: Grid Box 25Km
Location: -10.00, 48.00, 4.00, 61.00
Percentiles: 90.0
Probability Data Type: cdf

Medium-emissions scenario

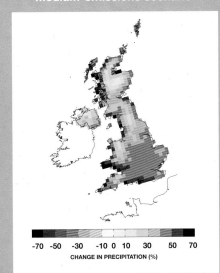

CHANGE IN PRECIPITATION (%)

Data Source: Probabilistic Land
Future Climate Change: True
Variables: precip_dmean_tmean_perc
Emissions Scenario: Medium
Time Period: 2070-2099
Temporal Average: DJF
Spatial Average: Grid Box 25Km
Location: -10.00, 48.00, 4.00, 61.00
Percentiles: 90.0
Probability Data Type: cdf

High-emissions scenario

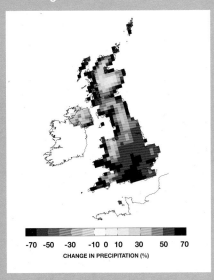

CHANGE IN PRECIPITATION (%)

Data Source: Probabilistic Land
Future Climate Change: True
Variables: precip_dmean_tmean_perc
Emissions Scenario: High
Time Period: 2070-2099
Temporal Average: DJF
Spatial Average: Grid Box 25Km
Location: -10.00, 48.00, 4.00, 61.00
Percentiles: 90.0
Probability Data Type: cdf

Figure 3.2. The Met Office's 2009 projections of the increases in winter rainfall by 2080 under three scenarios – low, medium and high greenhouse gas emissions. © UK Climate Projections 2009.

Low-emissions scenario

CHANGE IN PRECIPITATION ON THE WETTEST DAY (%)

Data Source: Probabilistic Land
Future Climate Change: True
Variables: precip_dmean_t99_perc
Emissions Scenario: Low
Time Period: 2030-2059
Temporal Average: DJF
Spatial Average: Grid Box 25Km
Location: -10.00, 48.00, 4.00, 61.00
Percentiles: 90.0
Probability Data Type: cdf

Medium-emissions scenario

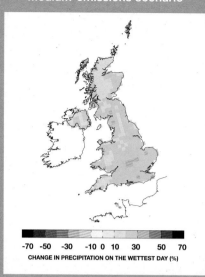

CHANGE IN PRECIPITATION ON THE WETTEST DAY (%)

Data Source: Probabilistic Land
Future Climate Change: True
Variables: precip_dmean_t99_perc
Emissions Scenario: Medium
Time Period: 2030-2059
Temporal Average: DJF
Spatial Average: Grid Box 25Km
Location: -10.00, 48.00, 4.00, 61.00
Percentiles: 90.0
Probability Data Type: cdf

High-emissions scenario

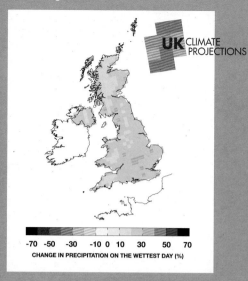

CHANGE IN PRECIPITATION ON THE WETTEST DAY (%)

Data Source: Probabilistic Land
Future Climate Change: True
Variables: precip_dmean_t99_perc
Emissions Scenario: High
Time Period: 2030-2059
Temporal Average: DJF
Spatial Average: Grid Box 25Km
Location: -10.00, 48.00, 4.00, 61.00
Percentiles: 90.0
Probability Data Type: cdf

Figure 3.3. The Met Office's 2009 projections of the increases in rainfall on the wettest day by 2040 under three scenarios – low, medium and high greenhouse gas emissions. © UK Climate Projections 2009.

Low-emissions scenario

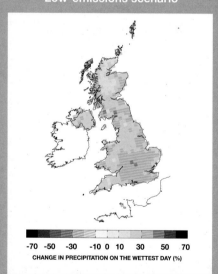

CHANGE IN PRECIPITATION ON THE WETTEST DAY (%)

Data Source: Probabilistic Land
Future Climate Change: True
Variables: precip_dmean_t99_perc
Emissions Scenario: Low
Time Period: 2070-2099
Temporal Average: DJF
Spatial Average: Grid Box 25Km
Location: -10.00, 48.00, 4.00, 61.00
Percentiles: 90.0
Probability Data Type: cdf

Medium-emissions scenario

CHANGE IN PRECIPITATION ON THE WETTEST DAY (%)

Data Source: Probabilistic Land
Future Climate Change: True
Variables: precip_dmean_t99_perc
Emissions Scenario: Medium
Time Period: 2070-2099
Temporal Average: DJF
Spatial Average: Grid Box 25Km
Location: -10.00, 48.00, 4.00, 61.00
Percentiles: 90.0
Probability Data Type: cdf

High-emissions scenario

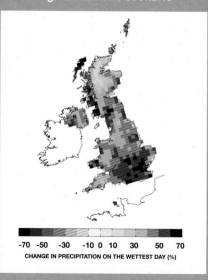

CHANGE IN PRECIPITATION ON THE WETTEST DAY (%)

Data Source: Probabilistic Land
Future Climate Change: True
Variables: precip_dmean_t99_perc
Emissions Scenario: High
Time Period: 2070-2099
Temporal Average: DJF
Spatial Average: Grid Box 25Km
Location: -10.00, 48.00, 4.00, 61.00
Percentiles: 90.0
Probability Data Type: cdf

Figure 3.4. The Met Office's 2009 projections of the increases in rainfall on the wettest day by 2080 under three scenarios – low, medium and high greenhouse gas emissions. © UK Climate Projections 2009.

The tops of groynes, perpendicular to the bank of the River IJssel, the Netherlands.

Making room for the river: the Netherlands

Water is the lifeblood of the Netherlands. In the south-east, the great arteries of the Rhine and the Meuse carry the rainwater of Europe into the country, dividing into tributaries and feeding the intricate veins of the Dutch canal network before emptying into the North Sea. The bright landscape of reflected light illuminates an ordered world of dikes, farms, peaceful settlements and slow-moving barges. A few windmills remain: the vital machinery that once pumped the marshes dry and kept the farms in business.

Ever since the Dutch first set out to master their low, translucent landscape, in the ninth century, their relationship with water has been intimate but ambivalent. Every metre of the way, the water is scrutinised and controlled. For although land reclamation, an advanced transport network and thriving ports brought prosperity, storms from the sea and swollen rivers from the east brought disaster, such as the 1421 St Elizabeth Deluge, when tens of thousands of people died. Traditionally, the Dutch response to such disaster has always been to build ever-better defences. Today these defences include 1,430km of river dikes, 1,017km of lake perimeter dikes and 690km of coastal dikes and dunes.[2]

The Netherlands is the best-protected river delta in the world. But there are costs involved in securing this level of protection. Dutch towns lurk behind the defences; rooftops appearing above the tops of the dikes. Seventy per cent of the gross domestic product of the Netherlands is generated below sea level. The land is densely populated – 465 people per square kilometre – but two-thirds of this land would be regularly flooded if there were no dikes. If the defences were to fail, either

Everywhere in the Netherlands there is evidence of centuries of careful stewardship of the watery landscape.

through a breach or through being overtopped, the consequences would be calamitous.

The last serious flood in the Netherlands was in 1953, when over 1,800 people perished as a spring tide and storm surge drove the sea through coastal defences. Today, however, the greater risk is from the other direction. In both 1993 and 1995 the inhabitants of the south of the Netherlands watched with mounting concern as the swollen Rhine and Meuse rose to the tops of the river dikes. The defences held but public confidence was seriously shaken. As climate change is predicted to bring heavier rainfall to the upper reaches of both rivers, the Dutch had no choice but to act to protect the country from an increasing threat of river flooding.

This time there was little appetite for building even higher dikes, not least because the higher any defence is built, the greater the penalty if it is ever breached. As so much of the land behind the dikes has been developed in modern times, this risk is unacceptable. Consequently, rather than trying to constrain the rivers further, the national water authority (the Rijkswaterstaat) developed a completely different strategy: working with the water and 'making room for the river'. The Ruimte voor de Rivier (Room for the River) project is complex and ambitious but the basic principle is simple: if there is more water in the river, space must be made for it to flow safely, at every single point along its route. If this means taking some defences down and returning land to marsh in order to cope with peak flows, so be it.

In practice, there are many ways of making room for a river. The most obvious is to move obstacles that obstruct the path of the river when it is in flood. For example, an embankment that carries a road or railway to a bridge over a river will cut across the floodplain and create a pinch point at the bridge which, in severe conditions, can lead to defences upstream of the bridge being overwhelmed. Puncturing the embankment creates more room for the river away from the bridge and so relieves the pinch point.

Groynes are a particularly common obstruction in Dutch rivers. These are man-made banks that protrude into the river and slow the flow at the edge. They are designed to concentrate the flow in the centre of the river, preventing it from silting up and thereby keeping it open to traffic, especially in summer when the water level is lower. Unfortunately the groynes also inhibit the flow of the river when it is in flood, so thousands of them are being lowered to a height that will let winter flood waters pass without seriously undermining their function in the summer.

The key measure of whether existing defences provide adequate room for the river is the capacity of water that they can hold. This is determined not only by the height of the dikes but also by the breadth and depth of the forelands between the river and the dikes, and by the depth of the river itself. Consequently, more room can be made for the river by deepening the river bed

Traditional flood protection: a farmhouse sits on its 'terp'.

A terrace lurks behind its dike.

and by deepening and widening the forelands. All of these options are being pursued at different points on the Rhine and the Meuse. They all involve major engineering works, not least the last option, which requires that the dikes themselves are repositioned further back from the river.

There are some points in the delta where development has been so extensive next to the river that none of these approaches is viable. In such circumstances either the dikes have to be raised or, preferably, a new route found for peak water flows. The latter option requires the creation of special flood channels that divert water around

the pressure points in the river before it returns to join the river downstream. This is difficult as land has to be sacrificed for the flood channel, but it is a more robust long-term solution than raising the barriers.

The most dramatic adjustments are planned for the Biesbosch, an area of polders (drained, reclaimed farmland) east of the city of Dordrecht that will be partly returned to marshland by the deliberate breach of defences. The Biesbosch is already a national park with extensive marshland, so this intervention will shift the balance between productive farmland and wildlife-rich

Top left: A railway embankment approaching a river bridge has been punctured to provide more room for the river in flood conditions.

Top right: The remains of a dike that has been deliberately moved to increase the width of the river foreland.

Bottom left and right: Much of the Biesbosch is already national park, but substantial areas of poldered farmland in the area are destined to become wetlands once again.

Flood walls for individual buildings are rarely an attractive solution to flood defence.

marsh. Nonetheless this is a radical move for a nation that has progressed over centuries by draining lakes and containing rivers. It will certainly be a huge change for the farmers who live there, some of whom will benefit from a special programme to raise, and in some cases move, entire houses affected by the project.

All these measures will increase the outlet capacity of the rivers from 15,000 cubic metres per second to 16,000 cubic metres per second. In the longer term, allowing for more substantial climate change effects, this capacity may be raised further to 18,000 cubic metres per second. The land that would have to be sacrificed to achieve this higher target has already been identified so that further development in these areas is minimised.

The Room for the River project builds on a long history of community-based action to control water and reduce flood risk in the Netherlands. The fundamental importance of flood prevention to everyone's lives and livelihoods has always encouraged cooperative approaches. As a result, the adaptation of individual houses has never been a high priority. There are, however, examples of adaptation in building design, above all the traditional 'terp', or artificial hillock, on top of which houses exposed to high flood risk are built. These tend to be individual farmhouses built near to rivers or in polders. An alternative, for houses built on the wrong side of dikes, is to build protective flood barriers around the building. The result may be effective but it is not attractive.

Floating homes in a new suburb of Utrecht.

There remains a radical approach to the adaptation of individual buildings that is gaining popularity in the Netherlands. Taking the principle of working with the water to its logical conclusion, several new developments have included houses with floating foundations. Tethered to the land and serviced by flexible ducts, these houses simply rise with the flood and fall again when the waters subside. The designs are innovative and costly but, in areas of high flood risk where new defences are prohibitively expensive, they offer a world of new opportunities.

The Dutch experience illuminates key facets of effective flood control. Above all, it is important to understand the river (or the tide) and the risks it presents. The health of a river is always changing. If these changes are not monitored, considered and addressed, the threat of flooding may quietly and invisibly increase. Those who live with water should never take it for granted.

Secondly, the Room for the River project demonstrates the value of working with water rather than against it, of building in flexibility for extreme conditions rather than building ever-higher defences. Defences are clearly essential to flood prevention but they are only half the story. In practice, there are many ways of articulating the relationship between land and water beyond the impermeable flood barrier. A corollary of this principle is that nowhere is completely off-limits to development on the basis of flood risk alone. The Dutch have built in the floodplain for centuries; this is possible if such development respects the long-term risks of its location, either by ensuring that there will always be enough room for the river or by designing the buildings themselves to be resilient to flood waters.

Thirdly, the existence of the Netherlands as a modern nation is testament to the importance of cooperative action in managing flood risk. Originally, many defences were built and maintained by community associations, but over time these responsibilities passed to local water boards supported by taxation. Although today the power of the Rijkswaterstaat is at some distance from local communities, this power is exercised in collaboration with regional and local authorities. Flood risk is nearly always a risk to communities rather than to single houses, so community solutions usually offer the best protection.

Finally, flood prevention can have multiple benefits. The Room for the River project is not exclusively concerned with flood prevention but also aims to improve the quality of the environment in the river basin, for wildlife and humans alike. For a population used to sheltering behind imposing dikes, the project is an opportunity to engage more creatively with the river landscape and enjoy its benefits. As flood-prevention measures always risk harming both the natural and the built environment, such a holistic approach is vital in order to maximise the potential for benefits for all.

The rolling hills of Britain

Britain was once part of the wide European mainland, conjoined with the modern Netherlands across a broad river basin. When the seas rose at the end of the last ice age this river basin was flooded and the islands of Britain took their modern form. The landscape of East Anglia still bears a striking similarity to its ancient neighbour across the North Sea: low and flat, crisscrossed by waterways and traditionally dependent on windmills to pump out the water and maintain the farmland. This, however, is where the similarity with the topography of the Netherlands ends.

Heading west from the Wash you cross the A1, the Grand Trunk Road linking London to the North, and the land begins to rise. Britain is a nation distinguished by its contours, from the gentle hills of the South Downs to the commanding crags of the Welsh and Scottish mountains. In Britain we expect rainwater to gather in the hills, flow into the rivers and empty out in the sea that surrounds us. We expect this to happen in an orderly fashion without interruptions or unexpected diversions. Floodplains are curiosities, odd features of the landscape with archaic functions. We do not expect floodplains actually to flood, for, like the Dutch, we have taken control of the rivers and expect them to do our bidding. Unlike the Dutch, however, few British citizens have a sense of the responsibilities and risks of living in a close relationship with water. Our houses do not shelter behind towering dikes but, wherever possible, open up to the river and celebrate the light and life of the water.

This riparian idyll is expressed in a thousand English villages, tucked into the folds of the landscape. Bucklebury is just such a village, a small settlement of 26 houses in Berkshire scattered along ancient field boundaries that converge on a twelfth-century Norman church, sitting amid a well-tended graveyard. Many of the houses have attractive gardens reaching down to the brook that runs through the village, the River Pang. The Pang was once vital to the livelihoods of the inhabitants of Bucklebury, driving waterwheels that powered both an iron foundry and a mill. Upstream the river was deliberately diverted and raised in order that these industries could get the most from their traditional renewable energy source. Today, however, the mill wheel is disintegrating and the foundry wheel adds character but no function to the house where once the blacksmith laboured.

In the days when the river had an important practical function, the inhabitants of Bucklebury would have paid it just as much attention as the wheels it turned. By 2007, however, such community stewardship and vigilance had long gone. Although there was a local history of flooding,

Bucklebury, an idyllic English village where gardens reach down to the seemingly gentle River Pang.

damage had never gone beyond a soggy football pitch, so no one took it upon themselves to monitor or maintain the river. Awareness of the risks of an increasingly weed-choked river was low.

The intense rains of July 2007 changed everything. The swollen Pang had nowhere to go so burst its banks. The rain was so heavy that a cascade of surface water also came from the other direction, running off the hills, down the road, across the fields and into the village. In a very short space of time 24 houses in the village were flooded and the church and graveyard were under water.

The villagers soon realised they were not going to be rescued by the emergency services, so set to work. After ensuring that all residents were safe, using all means available, they started the long-overdue task of clearing the river. It was several days before the waters had fully subsided, and by the time the people of Bucklebury were able to view the damage to their homes they had gained a collective spirit that would be crucial to the longer-term goal of preventing such devastation ever happening again. After a heated meeting in the local pub, the villagers decided that rather than expend their energy complaining

When these wheels powered the industry of the village, the villagers took more care of the river that their livelihoods depended on.

regular rota of weed clearance, built good working relationships with the local council (which has a responsibility for clearing culverts and gullies) and raised significant funds to enable the full implementation of their plan.

The components of this plan are striking in their simplicity. As in the much grander Dutch plan, the primary emphasis is not on building higher defences but on ensuring that excess water has room to flow without risk to property, even in extreme conditions. The most substantial measure is a new flood channel that will safely redirect the excess of a swollen River Pang behind the houses that front the river, rejoining the river downstream. Beyond this there are several smaller but nonetheless vital details. A new escape channel has been created for surface water so that it finds its way to a network of ditches rather than heading across the fields and into the heart of the village. New ditches have been dug to act as soakaways, absorbing as much water as possible when conditions are extreme. A key ditch wall has been strengthened to ensure that a rapid flow of surface water is kept inside it rather than overspilling and heading for homes – not least the two homes built in the 1960s right in the middle of the original local floodplain. In the longer term, the villagers hope that water meadows can be re-established upstream and downstream of the village to take up excess flow in the river and reduce the flooding risks for both Bucklebury and the villages beyond it.

to the authorities they would immediately begin the development of a flood-prevention strategy for the village. Whatever the failings of the local and national public bodies might have been, the people of Bucklebury realised that they would need the support of these bodies if a flood-prevention plan was to become a reality.

Twelve months and a great deal of effort later, Bucklebury had a detailed flood-prevention plan, key parts of which were already implemented. The villagers had also developed a keen awareness of the condition of the river, established a

In a relatively short space of time the relationship between the residents of Bucklebury and the river that defines the village has been transformed from passive neglect to active stewardship. Although the river no longer provides the power that underpins local incomes, it has reasserted and regained its place among the day-to-day concerns of the people who enjoy its charm. It may be harder to rebuild this relationship when the community at risk of flooding has 260 or 2,600 homes rather than the 26 in Bucklebury, but the stronger the community response, the more effective the final outcome is likely to be.

When the river burst its banks in 2007 almost all the houses in the village were flooded.

Top left: This seemingly innocuous roadside channel is designed to direct surface water into ditches. Previously, this water went over the road, through the gates, across the field and into the churchyard.

Top right: The river itself is kept free of choking weeds thanks to regular intervention by the villagers.

Bottom: A stronger wall for this watercourse removes the need for flood walls for the houses beyond.

Slow the rain

The importance of going with the flow rather than against it is increasingly recognised by planning authorities throughout Britain. In fact, the government consultation in 2004 that led to new guidelines for regional flood risk assessment was called 'Making space for water'. At every point along the journey of the British raindrop, there is a new interest in creating environments that reduce the risks of flooding. In the hands of more imaginative planners and designers, this interest becomes an opportunity to create new relationships between water resources and the built environment.

The increasing intensity of rainfall means that the free passage of water is a concern for everyone, not just river and coastal communities. Flash floods can happen anywhere, though they tend to occur in towns and cities, where the soft earth has been replaced by the hard, impermeable surfaces of tarmac, concrete and roof tiles. These surfaces gather every drop of rain and send them at high speed towards the drains, which can reach capacity all too soon. If storm drains are connected to sewers, the damage from flash floods when the drains fail can be particularly severe. In a typical British town, up to 40 per cent of surfaces are impermeable, with the result that 20-50 per cent of rainfall hits the drains immediately.[3]

Although it is possible to reduce the risk of flash floods by increasing the capacity of drains, this is a last resort. A far better approach is to slow the water down or capture it for later use. This is exemplified in the new development of Upton on the outskirts of Northampton, where rainwater storage has been successfully integrated into the urban environment, improving the quality of the public space along the way. Rainwater is channelled into a network of swales, substantial landscaped ditches that criss-cross the development, running down the centre of many streets.

The swales buffer the stormwater drains, filling up during periods of intense rain and then slowly releasing the accumulated water. Many are attractively planted and so also function as soft green centres to the streetscape – a welcome change from the hard lines of tarmac roads. Reedbeds on the edge of the development also help to take up excess rainwater during prolonged rainfall and so reduce the immediate burden on the swollen River Nene at the bottom of the hill. Furthermore, many of the houses have underground rainwater tanks that fill before rainwater from roofs is discharged into the swales.

The more a city is planted, the more permeable it is likely to be. Parks, tree-lined streets and domestic gardens all play an important role in protecting homes from flash floods. Yet this role has been under threat for some time as front gardens are paved over for cars and back gardens are turned into patios or sold off for development. This has become such a problem in London that planning permission must now be sought to create a hardstanding.[4] Yet almost any hard surface in the urban environment can be made permeable, absorbing rainwater and slowing the rush to the drains.

The concrete, tarmac and paving that dominate so many streets can all be replaced with permeable paving. This can take many forms, ranging from a strong plastic mesh through which plants are encouraged to grow to a traditional brick finish with specially designed pavers that let rainwater through to the ground below. At roof level, slate and concrete tiles can be replaced with earth and plants. A green roof with a decent depth of soil (100mm is a recommended minimum) will soak up the rainwater and release it into the drains once the first onslaught has passed.

Combine all these measures – swales, reedbeds and underground holding tanks; parks, trees and gardens; permeable paving and green roofs – and the soft urban landscape will cushion the inflexible drains from the severest of storms.

When the defences fail

Managing flood risk may be a new concern for the citizens of Northampton, but across Britain there are hundreds of communities that owe their

Top & bottom left: The suburb of Upton, Northampton, is criss-crossed by swales that contain and channel stormwater.

Bottom right: A reedbed on the edge of the development provides further stormwater buffering, reducing pressure on the River Nene.

Left: Permeable paving made from recycled plastic mesh filled with slate chippings.
Right: Flood walls create dead, unwelcoming public spaces.

survival and prosperity to historical flood prevention measures. These measures have typically been dominated by defensive strategies – building and maintaining walls – but here too a change of heart is under way. Planners and designers are increasingly working to a different tune, recognising that a more thoughtful and holistic approach to flood risk can be an opportunity to tear down the walls and create more integrated, liveable communities instead.

Located east of London in the county of Kent, Gravesend is an ancient river settlement that evolved at a point on the south bank of the Thames where the land rises out of the low marshland, thereby providing a decent landing point for river traffic just at the point where the river begins to open out into an estuary. The town flourished both as a commercial port and, in the nineteenth century, as an early tourist destination for Londoners who travelled via steamboat to enjoy its gardens and clean air.

Today Gravesend is reaping the benefits of its location at the heart of the Thames Gateway development, close to the new Ebbsfleet Eurostar station where high-speed trains head east to France. As part of the regeneration of the town a major development is planned for its dilapidated post-industrial riverbank, bringing new homes and businesses to the centre of the town. The

challenge for planners and architects is to achieve this in a manner that is flood-resilient but also maximises the value of the river for the new residents. Existing flood defences elsewhere in the town illustrate the problem for designers: heavy concrete barriers not only cut people off from the river, they also create dead, unwelcoming public spaces. Many recent developments simply lift living spaces to the first floor or higher, leaving the ground for cars. But this leaves the public realm barren – a network of passageways between parking spaces and gloomy undercrofts.

Gravesend rises out of the Thames floodplain. Although the elevation of the town protects much of its property, the riverside quarters are all at risk from flooding. The development at Albion Quayside by architects Kiran Curtis Associates is in flood zone 3a, which means that the area has a high probability of flooding: somewhere between once every 20 years and once every 100 years, not allowing for the effects of climate change. Add in up to a metre for rising seas and swollen rivers, and the design challenge changes. The new approach is to balance appropriate defences for everyday conditions with resilience in extreme conditions, i.e. a design that makes allowance for the defences being overtopped.

The site of the redevelopment at Albion Quayside is currently protected by a bleak flood-defence

Top: Making the ground level into a huge parking lot is a poor solution to flood risk.

Bottom: The proximity of this derelict industrial site to the rising Thames demands a radical approach to flood prevention in the development of Albion Quayside.

wall. This will be replaced by a terraced flood defence which will open up the river frontage to public view and create a riverbank where flora can flourish. If these flood terrace walls are over-topped, there are passages through to the interior of the site that will carry floodwaters to a green canal (ordinarily used as a swale for rainwater), a sacrificial area of the new public square and to the protected marina at the heart of the development. Each of these components has a primary function in the day-to-day life of the redeveloped public space but also provides excess capacity for floodwaters during extreme events.

The apartment blocks that front the river are designed such that all living spaces and essential building services are located above the highest level of flood risk but without a loss of connection to gardens and public space. As these apartments are likely to be isolated from higher ground during extreme flood conditions, there is a risk that inhabitants could be cut off. For this reason there are roof gardens above the car parks at the lowest level, which provide a point of access for emergency services, enabling evacuation. Although this flexibility in the design makes explicit the increasing flood risk faced by the settlement, it also potentially extends its life by decades.

There is a lesson here for all our efforts to design for the uncertain century ahead. If one of the effects of climate change is to increase the incidence of extreme conditions, we have to look beyond design thresholds (for homes, developments and cities) that are calamitous if exceeded and instead work out how we can survive and thrive even when our thresholds are occasionally breached.

This lesson is critical for those who want to build in the floodplain. Although government guidance now makes it clear that development should not take place on floodplains,[5] this guidance is of little relevance to established settlements such as Gravesend. Beyond Gravesend, the exceptions within the guidance are being fully exploited by the developers of the Thames Gateway, a new city in the ancient floodplain. If this city is to survive the century, the many professions involved in conjuring it out of the mud will have to be at least as diligent and creative as the redevelopers of Gravesend if they are to ensure that there is always room for the river alongside the many demands of human habitation. The Thames floodplain has long been compromised and obstructed, so its redevelopment through the Thames Gateway project is a golden opportunity to restore the floodplain's protective function for all the settlements in the area. This will require an infrastructure that can absorb rainwater and, more importantly, contain river and tidal waters in increasingly extreme conditions.

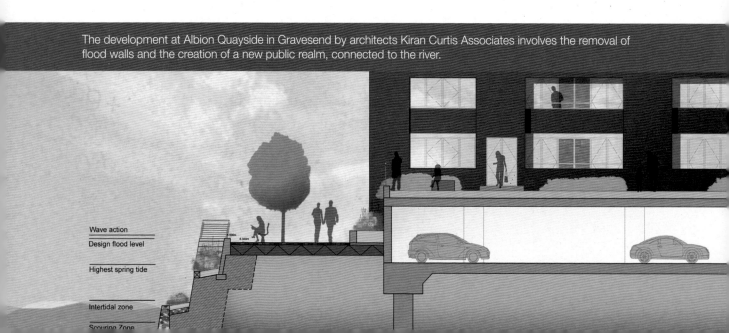

The development at Albion Quayside in Gravesend by architects Kiran Curtis Associates involves the removal of flood walls and the creation of a new public realm, connected to the river.

Wave action

Design flood level

Highest spring tide

Intertidal zone

Scouring Zone

An artist's impression of Albion Quayside, Gravesend. If the river embankment is overtopped, floodwaters will collect in the green swale, right of centre, and the protected marina.

Floodplains are being brought back to life elsewhere in Britain. Outside Milton Keynes, a new 'green corridor' is being created alongside the River Nene to recreate a 'forest floodplain'. Stormwater lakes within this corridor take up extra river capacity at peak times and become, in ordinary conditions, excellent sites for humans to play and wildlife to settle. In Lewisham, South London, the River Quaggy has been reclaimed from its culvert and now meanders through a beautiful new wetland park that can take up excess water and prevent flooding downstream. For a nation with a long-standing affection for messing about in boats, but which also values a dry hearth to return home to, this recreation of ancient river landscapes is the ultimate ecological win-win.

The flood-resilient home

However robust flood prevention may be at national, regional and community levels, there will always be individual houses exposed to a high risk of flooding. For their inhabitants, the challenge is to adapt the building so that, if and when the floodwaters do rise, damage is minimised and a return to normality can be made as quickly as possible. This involves both trying to keep the water out and making the inside of the house as resilient as possible for the unhappy occasions when the water does get in.

In the Suffolk town of Lowestoft, the Cotman Housing Association has completed a comprehensive retrofit of one its homes in order to demonstrate exactly what can be done to limit potential ruin. The house is sited in a small estate near to a watercourse with a history of flooding following heavy rains. The local council has reduced the flood risk for the estate as a whole by creating a holding pond between the watercourse and the road, so that the floodwaters have somewhere to go before they hit the streets. If the water does rise this far, an early-warning alarm in the street alerts the residents in their homes so that they can act quickly to protect their properties.

The house itself has a door guard that is inserted into a waterproof seal at the base of the door. Air bricks are also protected with temporary covers, and all the penetrations into the house that carry pipes and cables have been carefully sealed. Sewer pipes have non-return valves to prevent floodwaters backing up through the drains, and toilets and sinks have special bungs that are inserted as a second line of defence.

If floodwater gets through these defences, the interior of the house should suffer a minimum of damage. The floors and walls have hard, water-resistant finishes; skirting boards are designed to be quickly removed; doors can be lifted straight off their hinges and stored above the water; all the wiring is at ceiling height, with power points at dado height; and all electrical appliances are raised on plinths. Such a thorough retrofit may not be cheap, but the extra costs for new houses built in flood-risk areas are relatively small and manifestly worth paying.

If your home is so exposed to water that even these measures are likely to be inadequate, there is always the option of going with the flow. Near Hampton Court Palace on the Thames there is a small island community that has a long history of happy coexistence with the river. Like the new amphibious homes gaining in popularity in the Netherlands, all the houses on Taggs Island float, either directly on the river or in a small lagoon in the centre of the island. Each house is tethered to the island proper and services are provided through flexible ductwork. If the Thames is swollen by prolonged rainfall upstream, the island floods but the houses rise above the waters. The inhabitants may have to put their wellies on to leave their homes, but at least they can be assured of a dry home to return to, whatever the weather.

What you can do

First, assess your risk. The place to begin this task is the Environment Agency's flood-risk maps, which can be accessed online at www.environment-agency.gov.uk. However, do not assume that these maps are either comprehensive or accurate. The maps describe the risks of river and coastal flooding but not the risk of surface-water flooding, which is difficult to assess as intense rain can fall anywhere. If you are in a risk area, register with the Agency's flood warning scheme.

If you live near a river, investigate how well it is managed. Rivers are the responsibility of the Environment Agency, so again this is the best place to begin your enquiries. If you are not persuaded that the level of river management is satisfactory, consider developing a local programme of river monitoring and management. If you have the resources to do so, get an independent assessment of the local risk. Drainage channels, ditches and culverts are the responsibility of your local authority. If these are not in good condition, find out how often they are maintained. Lobby for a better service if you feel it is warranted.

Get advice from the National Flood Forum (www.floodforum.org.uk; helpline 01299 403055). Its *Blue Pages* is the first place to look for flood-proofing and flood-resilient products.

To reduce the risk of flash floods from intense rainfall, soften your landscape. Replace hard surfaces with porous surfaces, which will soak up the rain. Gardens, permeable paving, green roofs and soakaways all make a difference. Large rainwater tanks will also hold back water from the drains when the pressure is worst. Install wide gutters that can cope with intense rainfall.

The houses on Taggs Island on the River Thames are fully connected to mains services but rise and fall with the river.

If you want to protect your home from flooding, it is worth seeking professional advice to work out the best approach to defence. For example, you may be able to encircle your home with flood walls and floodgates. Alternatively, you may have to prepare for floodwater coming all the way up to your front door. If so, you need to ensure that every route into the building is blocked or can be blocked quickly, as follows.

- Seal all the gaps around pipework and cable sheathing.

- Install removable guards for doors.

- Put plastic covers on airbricks and expandable bungs in toilets, sinks and drains.

- Fit non-return valves on mains drains.

If you are at risk of prolonged exposure to flood-waters, you will need to protect your exterior walls as well. This could mean repointing brickwork or installing a waterproof membrane or render.

In order to minimise the damage and recovery time should floodwaters ever get past these defences, consider all the following options.

- Replace timber floors with concrete and use hard, waterproof finishes such as ceramic tiles on the ground floor.

- Finish your interior walls to dado height with waterproof render and paints.

- Rewire all ground-floor cabling at ceiling height, with sockets at dado height.

- Relocate your boiler and meters above the level of flood risk.

- Raise appliances on plinths.

- Install removable doors that can be lifted off their hinges.

- Store all valuables and paperwork out of harm's way.

If you think your home is about to be flooded, turn off all services at the mains and move everything you can to a higher level. 'Dry bags', designed for flood conditions, can be used to protect furniture.

The new landscape of Sutcliffe Park, South London, where the once-culverted River Quaggy now has space to flood before it reaches the town centre of Lewisham.

Chapter four
Drought

Climate change projections for the UK

Drought is an unfamiliar experience in the damp north-west of Europe, where rain from the Atlantic Ocean soaks the landscape on a regular basis. Yet the regularity of this rain is precisely what is threatened by climate change. Although there may be more rain in winter in the century ahead, it is likely that there will be a great deal less in summer.

Figure 4.1 shows the Met Office's 2009 projections for changes to summer rainfall by 2040 (from the 1961-1990 average) under the three scenarios for future global greenhouse gas emissions. As historic emissions are the principal driver of change up to this date, there is relatively little difference between the scenarios in 2040. Figure 4.2 shows the projected decreases to 2080, when the effects of our possible future emissions are clear. The maps illustrate the lower end of the range of rainfall projections, i.e. it is unlikely (only a 10 per cent chance) that rainfall will be lower, but it may well be higher. This end of the range, rather than the mid-range estimates, is shown because these are the conditions that we ought to be planning and building for today if we want to be sure our settlements will cope with the century ahead: decreases in summer rainfall of up to 50 per cent in the south by 2040 and up to 70 per cent by 2080, with 50 per cent reductions or more common throughout Britain under a high-emissions scenario. Even under a low-emissions scenario, there could be reductions in rainfall of up to 60 per cent in the south-west of England by 2080.

Annual rainfall is not expected to be seriously affected by climate change because decreases in summer rainfall are balanced by increases in winter rainfall (see overleaf). By 2040, no changes in annual rainfall are projected, though by 2080 some significant changes may be felt. Figure 4.3 shows the change in annual rainfall projected for 2040 for all three emissions scenarios. Figure 4.4 shows the projections for 2080. Under a high-emissions scenario, we could see reductions in annual rainfall of up to 20 per cent by 2080 on the south and west coasts of Britain and in the central belt of Scotland. Again, these maps illustrate the extreme end of the projections. As water reserves and reservoirs are mainly replenished during the winter months, summer drought may be manageable if the national water infrastructure is robust enough to cope with the shift in rainfall patterns. However, this may be difficult to achieve in practice. Water stored above ground in reservoirs will evaporate faster as temperatures rise and heatwaves become common, and underground water stores and aquifers may not benefit from the increase in winter rainfall as soils can absorb water only at a certain rate. The increased intensity of winter rainfall may lead to more surface run-off in winter rather than recharged groundwater.[1]

The sensitivity of Britain's hydraulic cycle to changes in the annual pattern of rainfall can be seen in projected changes to river flows. A detailed study of the likely impact of climate change on rivers in England and Wales by 2050 predicted decreases in flow of around 50 per cent in the summer and autumn months, with a fall of up to 80 per cent in some areas. During the winter months, river flows were projected to increase by up to 15 per cent. The number of months when the flow increases is expected to be less than the number of months when the flow decreases, so overall the annual flow will reduce, typically by between 10 and 15 per cent compared with today.[2] These changes could have consequences for water supplies as many aquifers are partially recharged by rivers.

Beyond these supply-side problems, a great deal more pressure on the water supply can be expected in the south as a result of a growing population and more homes, businesses, industry, horticulture and agriculture. Although water slips through our fingers every day, its preciousness will become ever more apparent as the century progresses.

Low-emissions scenario

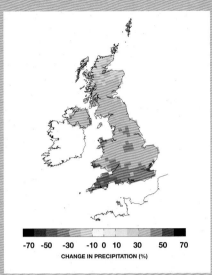

Medium-emissions scenario

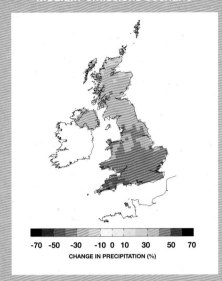

High-emissions scenario

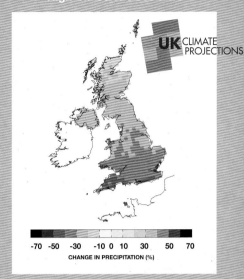

Data Source: Probabilistic Land
Future Climate Change: True
Variables: precip_dmean_tmean_perc
Emissions Scenario: Low
Time Period: 2030-2059
Temporal Average: JJA
Spatial Average: Grid Box 25Km
Location: -10.00, 48.00, 4.00, 61.00
Percentiles: 10.0
Probability Data Type: cdf

Data Source: Probabilistic Land
Future Climate Change: True
Variables: precip_dmean_tmean_perc
Emissions Scenario: Medium
Time Period: 2030-2059
Temporal Average: JJA
Spatial Average: Grid Box 25Km
Location: -10.00, 48.00, 4.00, 61.00
Percentiles: 10.0
Probability Data Type: cdf

Data Source: Probabilistic Land
Future Climate Change: True
Variables: precip_dmean_tmean_perc
Emissions Scenario: High
Time Period: 2030-2059
Temporal Average: JJA
Spatial Average: Grid Box 25Km
Location: -10.00, 48.00, 4.00, 61.00
Percentiles: 10.0
Probability Data Type: cdf

Figure 4.1. The Met Office's 2009 projections of the changes to summer rainfall by 2040 under three scenarios – low, medium and high greenhouse gas emissions. © UK Climate Projections 2009.

Low-emissions scenario

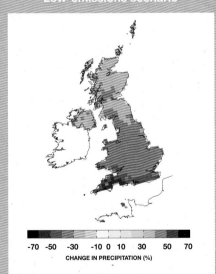

Medium-emissions scenario

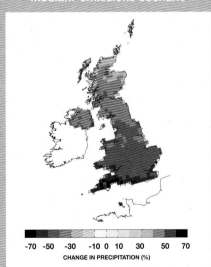

High-emissions scenario

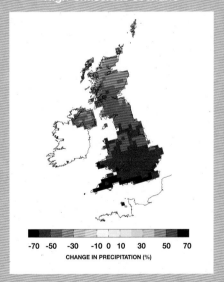

Data Source: Probabilistic Land
Future Climate Change: True
Variables: precip_dmean_tmean_perc
Emissions Scenario: Low
Time Period: 2070-2099
Temporal Average: JJA
Spatial Average: Grid Box 25Km
Location: -10.00, 48.00, 4.00, 61.00
Percentiles: 10.0
Probability Data Type: cdf

Data Source: Probabilistic Land
Future Climate Change: True
Variables: precip_dmean_tmean_perc
Emissions Scenario: Medium
Time Period: 2070-2099
Temporal Average: JJA
Spatial Average: Grid Box 25Km
Location: -10.00, 48.00, 4.00, 61.00
Percentiles: 10.0
Probability Data Type: cdf

Data Source: Probabilistic Land
Future Climate Change: True
Variables: precip_dmean_tmean_perc
Emissions Scenario: High
Time Period: 2070-2099
Temporal Average: JJA
Spatial Average: Grid Box 25Km
Location: -10.00, 48.00, 4.00, 61.00
Percentiles: 10.0
Probability Data Type: cdf

Figure 4.2. The Met Office's 2009 projections of the changes to summer rainfall by 2080 under three scenarios – low, medium and high greenhouse gas emissions. © UK Climate Projections 2009.

Low-emissions scenario   **Medium-emissions scenario**   **High-emissions scenario**

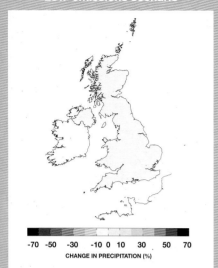

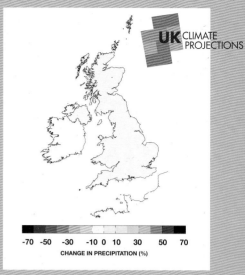

Figure 4.3. The Met Office's 2009 projections of the change in annual rainfall by 2040 under three scenarios – low, medium and high greenhouse gas emissions. © UK Climate Projections 2009.

Low-emissions scenario   **Medium-emissions scenario**   **High-emissions scenario**

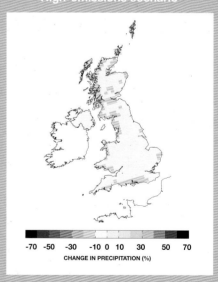

Figure 4.4. The Met Office's 2009 projections of the change in annual rainfall by 2080 under three scenarios – low, medium and high greenhouse gas emissions. © UK Climate Projections 2009.

The streets of Fira, Santorini, Greece.

Surviving and thriving with rainwater: Santorini

Santorini is the southernmost island of the Cyclades, the group of arid, sunburnt islands scattered across the Aegean Sea between mainland Greece and Crete. It is famous both as a popular tourist destination, offering a near-perfect whitewashed Mediterranean idyll, and as a destroyer of civilisations. For Santorini is the extant rim of the caldera, or supervolcano, that last exploded around 3,500 years ago with calamitous consequences for all the inhabitants of the Aegean. The Minoan civilisation, centred on Crete, did not recover.

The sophisticated Minoan outpost on Santorini itself was wiped out by the volcano and the island completely covered in ash and rock. Half a millennium later, however, the island was thriving again, settled in turn by Phoenicians, Greeks and Romans. Its strategic position in the centre of the south Aegean meant that it was always likely to attract settlers, but its value to traders and military campaigners did not bring a surfeit of prosperity and development. An isolated volcano in the middle of the sea is no place to build a grand mercantile city, especially when the most basic need of all human settlements – water – is in short supply.

Santorini has no rivers or underground water reserves and low seasonal rainfall: less than 370mm, almost all of which falls between October and April.[3] In the summer the temperature never gets unbearable, thanks to the cooling effect of the sea, which also humidifies the air, but a

The town of Fira perches on the crater's edge of the ancient supervolcano.

pleasant climate is little compensation for drought. The people who decided to settle on Santorini had to face this harsh reality and be ingenious: they had to trap, collect and store rainwater in the winter and use it with the greatest of care throughout the rest of the year. 'Rainwater harvesting' may not have been invented on Santorini, but it reached a level of sophistication that has rarely been matched, defining the form and details of entire buildings.

In the ninth century BCE a Greek settlement was established high on a hilltop in the south-east of the island. Although the site is a long climb from sea level and was evidently chosen for reasons of defence rather than everyday practicality, the town flourished for centuries, in time becoming absorbed into the Roman Empire. The view from the steps of the amphitheatre is suitably dramatic:

the deep blue of the Aegean Sea fading into the bright sky. The archaeological remains of the town illustrate the central role that water played in the Roman household. The focus of the home was the atrium or inner courtyard, at the centre of which was the impluvium or basin. The roofs of this courtyard sloped inwards, towards the impluvium, with the impluvium itself open to the sky. Thus the rainwater was all directed to the centre of the room and into the primary collecting chamber. A drainage pipe from the impluvium led to an underground cistern. Many of these cisterns still fill with rainwater today, albeit without the assistance of well-placed roofs and gutters.

This architectural form was integral to Roman villas across the empire and influenced the courtyard house that is still common in Mediterranean and Middle Eastern cities (see page 31). Although the

Flowers flourish in the humid air.

The remains of a Roman impluvium in Old Thera. Rainwater drained from the roofs into the central basin, which in turn fed underground tanks.

form did not last as a rainwater-harvesting system on Santorini, the basic design principle of storing winter rainwater in a large cistern underneath the dwelling survived and is still in use today.

All houses are designed to shed water. Keeping the rain out and the hearth dry is perhaps the most fundamental function of any dwelling, from basic benders to sophisticated modern homes. The collection of rainwater ought, therefore, to be entirely compatible with this function. If rain is being directed and channelled, only one more design step is needed to channel it somewhere useful. Yet this extra step is rarely made; only when drought conditions prevail is it undertaken as a matter of course.

Because buildings of all kinds are rainwater channellers it is not immediately obvious that the houses of Santorini extend this function to rainwater collection. You have to look carefully when wandering the streets of the island's small settlements to see the tell-tale signs. The access hatches for the underground cisterns are the easiest to spot. The hatch is typically sited at the edge of a courtyard with a hole providing drainage into the tank and a lid enabling the owner to access and service it.

The priority of water in building design becomes more evident on closer inspection of many of the older houses. Typically, the house sits proud on the hillside with the basement space given over to the large rainwater tank. The courtyard and roof

have perimeter walls, including small upstands at thresholds, to ensure that no rainwater escapes. All water is directed to the underground tank, usually through holes in the courtyard floor. Water quality is maintained, as far as possible, by the limestone of the tank walls, the exclusion of light and an annual clean (today, chemicals may also be added). Traditionally, toilets are located away from the house with their own basement composting chambers, which are emptied periodically on to the fields.

Simple really. In fact, this approach to coping with drought conditions is so simple and effective that it sustained human society on Santorini for millennia. But not any more: modern life and especially modern tourism demand a great deal more water than the heavens above Santorini can provide.

In the second half of the twentieth century Santorini underwent a remarkable transformation from an impoverished island, its economy struggling to recover from a devastating earthquake in 1956, to a prosperous and highly regarded tourist destination. This was achieved without the character and landscape of the island being despoiled. Santorini has managed to square the tourist circle, retaining its charm and beauty while also benefiting from the spending of up to a million visitors per year.

The familiar architecture of tourism is now ubiquitous across the island: hotels and villas, restaurants

A typical house on Santorini, sitting above a large tank that collects the limited rainwater that falls on the building's roofs and courtyard. The washroom stands apart from the house above its own chamber.

and shops, sundecks and swimming pools. Tourists may bring wealth but they are the anti-thesis of the traditional, frugal Santorinian: their primary goal is not to conserve but to consume. Consequently Santorini has had to adapt, above all in radically increasing its water supply.

The water supply in Santorini is now secured by imports, delivered by ferry from the Greek mainland, and by a desalination plant. The plant sits on the cliff top just outside the town of Oia, at the northern tip of the crescent island. Seawater is drawn up a pipe from the ocean below and driven through the energy-intensive 'reverse osmosis' process (it takes about 5kWh of energy to produce one cubic metre of desalinated water at Oia[4]). The output is either piped to dwellings or delivered in trucks. Many of the new hotels

have large water tanks in their basements in the manner of the older houses, though these tanks are filled not by rainwater but by desalinated seawater, replenished as often as twice a week in the high season.

The old rainwater tanks are still used, at least by some, but their importance has declined as demand for water has increased. The problem with having a seemingly endless supply of water is that you no longer have to worry about how you consume it; if the tank will never run dry, you can confidently splash out. As demand for water soars, the relative contribution of rainwater to meeting this demand inevitably diminishes.

The daily financial costs of shipping and desalin-ating so much water are borne by the local people

Courtyard hatches are clues to
basement rainwater tanks.

so it may be that demand for water falls as both
oil supplies and tourist numbers dwindle. If and
when demand for water does fall, rainwater may
once again become a vital part of the everyday
lives of the people of Santorini. Assuming, of
course, that the rain continues to fall.

A city as rainwater collector

This story of transition from water self-sufficiency
to dependence and vulnerability is not unique to
Santorini; it is repeated in arid regions across the
world. Whole cities have undergone similar
transformations, nowhere more comprehensively
than in Jodhpur, the great city of the Thar desert
in Rajasthan, north-west India. The tragedy in
Jodhpur is that the path back to self-sufficiency
has long been destroyed.

When Rao Jodha founded the city in the fifteenth
century, he chose a site that had maximum potential for harvesting rainwater. In doing so, he was
drawing on thousands of years of experience, a
history that included many periods of climate
change when monsoons failed and ever more
demands were placed on the ingenuity of the
water engineers of the northern deserts.[5] The city
is situated at the edge of a rocky plateau, which
provided the main catchment for the water supply.
Long canals were built to collect rainwater and
transport it to the city, where it was stored in many
tanks. Elaborate wells tapped the water that seeped
from the tanks as well as the limited groundwater.
Individual houses incorporated simple rainwater
tanks to collect whatever fell on their roofs.

In the twentieth century the entire catchment for
the city's rainwater tanks was destroyed by
quarrying. Now the rains fill the quarries rather
than the canals, and the canals themselves have
been filled with rubble. The canals inside the city
are choked with garbage and the household tanks
have fallen into disrepair. The decorated underground step wells have also become dumping
grounds for municipal waste. The city's water is
now piped in from far beyond the desert, but the
cost has been high and long-term water security

and the tourists. There is, however, a more
profound cost inherent in this transformation of
the water supply: a loss of independence and an
increase in vulnerability. When in 2007 a ship sank
in the bay and started leaking diesel oil into the
sea, there was a very real threat that the desalination plant would be contaminated and put out of
action, just at the point when the tourist season
was reaching its peak. The crisis was averted but
the island's vulnerability was exposed.

Santorini's dependence on oil to deliver and
produce its water will become an ever-increasing
problem in the course of the twenty-first century.
There are alternatives, such as wind- and solar-
powered desalination, which will look increasingly attractive as oil prices rise. On a remote
Aegean island, however, oil is just as critical to the
transport of tourists as it is to the supply of water,

Top left: Modern Santorini is dependent on the tourist trade, so demand for water has rocketed.

Top middle: Pipes from the ocean draw water up to the energy-intensive desalination plant, which the islanders now depend on for their water supply.

Top right: New hotels in Santorini also have basement water tanks, but these are filled by regular deliveries from the desalination plant.

Above: A near-derelict church sits above its substantial rainwater tank. There is now little incentive to maintain these tanks on the island.

has been undermined. Unfortunately for the people of Jodhpur, the decimation of the landscape itself means that the remarkable works of the city's early water engineers will never be brought back to life.[6]

A country as rainwater collector

In Britain, local rainwater collection has never been a primary feature of the water supply. In the days when water was sourced locally, people turned to rivers and wells rather than to their rooftops. Britain has, however, been through the same transformation as Santorini – from localised water supplies, which users understood and managed themselves, to a regional infrastructure that appears to satisfy unlimited demand. Unlike in Santorini this is not a recent change; most of the great reservoirs that supply England (many of them in Wales) were built by the Victorians.

The Victorian water infrastructure of England is a far cry from the energy-intensive infrastructure required to supply modern Santorini. Most of the movement of rainwater from the hills to the reservoirs and thence to the pipes is driven by gravity, that most benign of all earthly powers. Energy is required to pump and process water along the way, but this is a relatively small input to the otherwise wholly natural hydraulic cycle, the great movement of water vapour from the land and seas to the sky, then back to the land as rain and so through the earth and the intricate tapestry of the man-made water infrastructure to the sea once again. Our success in exploiting this cycle is easy to undervalue, for the renewable energy that drives the hydraulic cycle does not have to be caught by wind turbines or trapped by solar panels. The rain continues to fall, without any intervention by us.

The only difficulty arises when the hydraulic cycle fails to meet the ever-increasing demands of the humans that stand in its way. This is already a problem in the south-east of England, which, despite the country's rainy reputation, is one of the most water-stressed regions of Europe because of the extent and density of the development of London and the region as a whole. Water restrictions are already familiar following sustained winter and summer droughts. As the century progresses, the pressure on the mains supply will become ever more intense. The only way to reduce this pressure and keep the region within the limits of the shrinking hydraulic cycle is to cut demand for mains water.

At the household level there are two main ways of reducing demand for mains water: using water more efficiently and supplementing mains water with rainwater. It is also possible to recycle water, though the scope for this is limited (see overleaf). Although there is enormous potential for improving water efficiency in the profligate homes of England, most of which still do not have water meters, water efficiency alone will not be enough to cope with the increasing stress on the water supply.[7] Domestic rainwater collection, in one form or another, will have to become a more prominent part of our water supply. Coping with drought then becomes a collective effort, combining national supply with well-designed dwellings and careful inhabitants.

The Green House in East Sussex is just such a well-designed dwelling, occupied by careful and considerate owners Nicholas and Heather Worseley. When Nicholas bought the house in 2005, it was a dishevelled and unloved old hulk, desperately in need of repair. The subsequent renovation by BBM Sustainable Design Ltd was an opportunity for Nicholas to express his commitment to ecological design in every detail of the specification. The result is an attractive, energy-efficient home that demands little from the mains water infrastructure.

The house is substantial; Nicholas and Heather were looking for something smaller but they wanted a large garden and so have ended up with a large house. This, however, is an advantage for their water specification, for there is an abundance of roof space from which to collect and channel rainwater. The rainwater is collected in an underground tank with a capacity of 4,000 litres,

The Green House in East Sussex, renovated by BBM Sustainable Design Ltd.

installed as part of their renovation. Although the installation of such a large tank is complex, once in place it disappears from view. Crucially, unlike ordinary water butts, the tank is big enough to see through a prolonged drought without running dry. This means that it will ease demand on the mains water supply at just the point when the mains water infrastructure is most stressed.

Nicholas and Heather still use mains water but only for drinking, cooking and personal washing. The rainwater is used for the garden, for flushing toilets and for washing clothes. This division of tasks between the main supply and the supply from the roof means that demand for mains water is reduced without the complex filtration needed to turn rainwater into regulation-approved drinking water. Demand for both water sources is reduced by the use of water-efficient fittings within the home, such as low-flush toilets, aerating taps (which mix the water with air to give a full flow for less water) and a water-efficient washing machine. The biggest single demand for water, in the summer at least, is the vegetable garden. The rainwater-fed pond, a haven for electric blue dragonflies, has so far survived without the need for topping up.

Living with a rainwater collection system has made Nicholas and Heather conscientious about saving water. The tank reminds them of the value and constraints of their water supply and so encourages more careful behaviour. Nicholas checks the level of the tank every day on a simple wall-mounted gauge and is quick to act if there is any indication that the level is dropping faster than expected – an indication of a leak somewhere in the house. This attentiveness to the water supply and appreciation of the preciousness of water is a far cry from the attitude of most British households, whose unmetered mains supply gives no sense of the limitations of the water supply and no incentive to take care in the use of water. One way or another – through metering, pricing, efficiency standards and rainwater collection – these households will have to change their ways as the century progresses, learning to value the life-giving liquid that we all too easily take for granted.

Keeping the garden growing

The biggest stress on the mains water supply occurs in the height of summer, when hundreds of thousands of households turn on their hose-pipes to water their gardens. Collecting rainwater to provide for your garden is therefore an excellent way of reducing the effects of drought. Although garden rainwater tanks come in a particularly wide variety of shapes and sizes, bigger is better for drought resistance as small tanks are likely to run out during prolonged periods without rain, just when you need the water most.

Another option for gardens is 'grey water', the stuff that comes out of your shower, bath, basin and washing machine (but not toilet). This cannot be stored for long as it soon starts to get smelly, so the best place to recycle it is the garden. This part of the system can be relatively easy to retrofit if the pipes from these water sources run outside your house. With a little extra plumbing, these can be redirected to simple underground irrigation systems made from plastic pipes. However, pipes from baths, showers and washing machines should first be redirected to a simple holding tank, which will prevent lots of water hitting the garden at once. A filter inside this tank, such as a straw bale, will reduce the solids entering and potentially disrupting the irrigation system. The straw can be removed every few months and composted.[8]

The simplest way to cope with long, dry summers in the garden is to mulch. Adding a thick, organic top dressing to the soil will help the soil to retain moisture as well as suppress weeds. Similarly, the more compost you can make and dig in to the soil, the more the soil structure will improve, enhancing the ability of the soil to hold on to water.

Above all, choose your plants with care. The potential of 'dry gardening' has been amply demonstrated by Beth Chatto in her stunning garden in drought-prone Essex. Chatto's dry garden stands in the long English tradition of international plant-collecting and gardening,

Left, centre left & centre: Every down-pipe from the substantial roofs feeds an underground tank.

Right: Owners Nicholas and Heather combine careful use of mains water with rainwater harvesting.

Centre right: All taps have aerators that give a full flow for less water.

Bottom left: The garden is the principal beneficiary of the rainwater tank, though this pond survives without topping up.

Bottom right: A meter indicates the level of the rainwater tank and helps to sustain Nicholas's and Heather's frugality.

employing plants from arid regions across the world. The result is a rich mix of silvers, glaucous blues, yellows and pinks, left to flourish under the hot summer sun without any regular watering.

Shifting clays

Prolonged drought can have profound effects on ground conditions, especially clay soils, which are liable to dry out. As clay dries it contracts, cracking pipes and rocking foundations. As there are large swathes of clay soils in the south-east of England, not least in London, this could prove to be one of the most costly impacts of climate change over this century.

Unfortunately, subsidence and cracking are triggered not only by the soil shrinkage brought on by drought but also by the swelling caused by prolonged rainfall. Consequently the anticipated combination of increased winter rains and frequent summer drought could be particularly damaging. According to the British Geological Survey, shrinkage and heave have already had huge impacts in Britain, costing the economy an estimated £3 billion over the past decade.[9]

Any new house built on clay soil can be specified to withstand severe shrinkage and heave. For masonry buildings, this can be achieved by using deeper foundations that extend into more stable soils. Alternatively, pad foundations can be used with timber-frame construction. The advantage of timber-frame design is the innate flexibility of the material, unlike concrete blocks and brick, which will crack under pressure. However, most of the future subsidence problems brought on by summer drought and winter rains are likely to be with houses that are already standing, many of which have simple, shallow foundations that offer little protection against severe ground movements. The only guaranteed way to protect a property against subsidence is underpinning, but this is inevitably a complex and expensive process. An alternative approach is to improve the ground rather than the structure that sits in it. If the cause of the subsidence is the swing in moisture content

between winter and summer, this can be relieved by maintaining a high moisture content throughout the year – by making all ground surfaces permeable, trapping rainwater before it runs off, and directing rainwater into the ground rather than the drains by using soakaways.

Vegetation has an important role to play in reducing surface water run-off, especially in summer when water is most needed and rainwater is liable to head straight for the drains because the ground at this time is so dry. A house surrounded by a richly planted garden will be much less likely to subside than a house surrounded by concrete or paving. However, vegetation in the form of trees can also exacerbate soil shrinkage if they demand too much water for themselves. This has led to the unhappy situation of insurance companies routinely requiring the removal of trees as part of the management of subsidence claims. Although this may be justified when the tree is a particularly thirsty species (poplars are the worst offenders), as a blanket safety-first policy it is potentially disastrous for urban environments, given the vital roles trees play in cooling, cleaning and enriching the street scene.

In 2008 the London Tree Officers Association published the 'Joint Mitigation Protocol', a method of dealing with subsidence claims where trees are threatened, which properly values the contribution trees make to the urban environment and promotes remedial pruning as a realistic alternative to felling. The protocol, negotiated with the insurance industry, was an important step forward in protecting the green infrastructure of the capital. In the longer term this needs to be combined with more active management of trees, including regular pruning where trees present a possible risk to properties on clay soils.

What you can do

If the national water-supply infrastructure is to become more resilient to prolonged drought, we have to learn to live with less. Unfortunately there is little incentive in a centralised system for any individual household to take action, especially if its water is not metered. So if you do not have a water meter, ask for one to be installed. Then your community-minded actions to save water will at least have some direct benefits for you in reduced costs. Consider all of the following.

- Fix any taps that are dripping. When replacing taps, install taps with aerating heads.

- Add just the right size of plastic bottle to your toilet cistern to keep it working well with less water. Alternatively, retrofit a device inside your cistern which allows you to flush just as much as you need, keeping the handle pressed. When replacing a toilet, install an ultra-low-flush model (2 litres / 4 litres dual flush).

- Use low-flow or aerating shower heads. Avoid power showers, which can use more water than baths.

- When replacing a washing machine or dishwasher, check for water efficiency as well as energy efficiency.

If you use water outside for any purpose (gardening and car washing are the usual culprits), use

Beth Chatto's stunning dry garden in Essex.

rainwater. To prevent your supply running out just as a drought is kicking in, install the biggest tank that you can afford and can squeeze in. Reduce your need for water in the garden by mulching, planting drought-tolerant plants and using grey water (see page 88).

If you are undertaking a major renovation or building project, consider installing a large underground rainwater tank to supply the toilets and washing machine as well as the garden. This will see you through periods of prolonged drought.

If your house is built on clay soil, expose as much of the garden to the rain as possible, using permeable paving where appropriate (see page 64). Plant up as much of your land as you can to help retain rainwater. If possible, direct the outflow of gutters and downpipes into ditches and soakaways. Avoid planting tree species that are known for their thirst. If you are building on clay soil, make sure your foundations are deep enough, or your design flexible enough, to cope with regular contraction and heave in the soil.

A garden designed to be drought-tolerant need be no less exuberant than the traditional English cottage garden.

The bigger the tank for your garden, the better.

Chapter five
Threatened coasts

Climate change projections for the UK

The cities, towns and villages that line the coast and estuaries of Britain have long flourished thanks to the gifts of the sea: food, transport, trade and tourism. But living on the fragile boundary of land and sea has always had its risks. Storm surges, coastal erosion and swollen rivers have brought disaster many times over in the course of Britain's history. Today, these risks are compounded by an inescapable consequence of climate change: rising sea levels.

The islands of Britain were created as a result of sea-level rise at the end of the last ice age, when vast quantities of water from melting glaciers poured into the oceans, flooding Doggerland, the broad plain joining Britain to mainland Europe. The ice had been so thick and heavy that the land under it was compressed. When the ice disappeared, this land started a slow rebound that is with us still – the north-west of the country rising and the south-east sinking. This rebalancing of the island means that today's rising seas will have different effects in different parts of the country.

Twenty-first century sea-level rise is also driven, in part, by melting ice. Huge quantities of water are stored in the Greenland and Antarctic ice sheets, with smaller amounts in other ice caps and glaciers. Meltwater is currently pouring into the sea from all these sources, to a greater or lesser extent (ice that is already in the sea, such as in Arctic icebergs, does not increase sea levels when it melts). However, the biggest driver of sea-level rise is the thermal expansion of the existing ocean in response to rising global temperatures. The estimates of global sea-level rise produced by the Intergovernmental Panel on Climate Change (IPCC) assume that 70 per cent of sea-level rise in the twenty-first century will be as a result of this factor alone. In its 2007 assessment, the IPCC estimated that global sea level will rise by between 18cm and 59cm by the end of the century.[1] But the rise in any region is also determined by other factors: not only land movement but also ocean circulation, temperature and salinity.

The Met Office's 2009 projections of sea-level rise around Britain[2] were based on the IPCC's 2007 estimates. Table 5.1 shows the projections of absolute sea-level rise (i.e. not including land movement) around the coastline of Britain by the end of the century. As in the IPCC's estimates, these projections take account of both the thermal expansion of the ocean and the melting of ice in glaciers, ice caps and ice sheets. The variability in the projections is principally due to different assumptions about how much ice will melt. The upper-range projection for a high-emissions scenario is a rise of three-quarters of a metre.

Figure 5.1 shows how this absolute rise in sea level translates into relative rises around the rebalancing coastline of Britain. The map illustrates the central estimate for a medium-emissions scenario. The differences within Table 5.1 can be used to adjust for different scenarios. For example, the difference between the central estimate of the medium-emissions scenario and the upper estimate of the high-emissions scenario is 38.9cm. This means that in East Anglia and the south-west of England, where Figure 5.1 indicates a rise of up to 50cm, the upper estimate of relative sea-level rise for a high-emissions scenario is approaching 90cm. The north-west of Scotland will be the least affected.

These projections take account of the fact that there has been an acceleration in the flow of meltwater from the edges of the major ice sheets. There is real concern that this acceleration could increase, leading to much larger rises in sea level than those predicted. This concern is informed both by current evidence of change in meltwater flows and by geological evidence from the last interglacial period, 125,000 years ago, when ice sheets were similar to those today, temperatures similar to those projected for the century ahead, and sea levels rose by up to 2.4m.[3] In its 2009 projections, the Met Office drew on all this evidence to define a 'High++' scenario – an unlikely but possible future for Britain this century. In this scenario, sea-level rise is somewhere between 93cm and 1.9m, which could result in an extreme upper water level of 3m under storm conditions. The top end of this range is highly unlikely, but if it did come to pass its impact would be devastating. For those involved in protecting the coastline of Britain, and those living there, such low probability / high cost scenarios cannot be ignored.

Table 5.1. Projected absolute sea-level rise over the twenty-first century (cm).[4]

	Lower estimate	Central estimate	Upper estimate
Low emissions	11.6	29.8	48
Medium emissions	13.1	36.9	60.7
High emissions	15.4	45.6	75.8

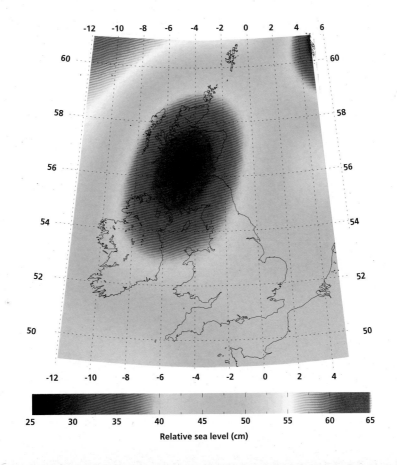

Figure 5.1. Projected relative sea-level change (cm) around the UK over the twenty-first century.[5] © UK Climate Projections 2009.

The low, scrubby island of Torcello, an unpromising landscape on which to build a grand city.

Living with the sea at your door: the city of Venice

Venice has a beauty and mystery quite unlike any other city in the world. The architecture, elegant and flamboyant in equal measures, is illuminated by an ever-changing, often dazzling light. But it is something beyond the buildings themselves that creates the unique, mesmerising effect: the city's manifest vulnerability. The murky green waters of the Grand Canal lap at the stained steps of the *palazzi*, every wave a reminder of the unlikely and precarious survival of the glittering buildings above.

The city of Venice is built on a tiny archipelago of islands, the Rivus Altus, in the middle of a broad, shallow lagoon. The first significant settlement in the lagoon, in the seventh century, was built further north on the island of Torcello, but was abandoned five centuries later. Today the Byzantine cathedral of Santa Maria Assunta still stands in the centre of Torcello but, for the most part, the island is an image of what the early Venetians set to work upon to create their magical city: low, scrubby marshland, barely rising above sea level. With such a starting point, it is no wonder the city is described as miraculous.

The Venetian lagoon has an area of 550km^2 and is home to dozens of islands and large areas of salt marsh. Its fragile ecosystem is the product of the mainland drainage basin that feeds it from the west and the tides of the Adriatic Sea to the east, which flush the lagoon twice every day. The lagoon is protected from the full force of the sea by the islands of the littoral (which stretch 60km from the mouth of the River Adige in the north to the mouth of the River Piave in the south), a thin line of sand, sunny villas and the occasional grand hotel, broken by the three inlets to the lagoon where tides and traffic make their way. The lagoon itself is shallow, with an average depth of only 1.2 metres, so passageways for boats are clearly marked out with *bricole* – bound posts driven into the sea floor. Deeper channels have been cut to allow cruise ships to reach the port of Venice and oil tankers to reach the industrial complex of Porto Marghera, built on reclaimed land on the western bank of the lagoon.

Despite the protection of the littoral, life in the centre of the lagoon has always been at the mercy of the tide, especially when this is strengthened by storm surges in the Adriatic. The people of Venice may have found that the peculiar topography of the place offered them protection, autonomy and ultimately maritime power, but the price they have always paid is regular tidal flooding. Over the years rivers have been diverted, flood

defences built, and quays and pavements raised and raised again. Look carefully and the evidence of this rebuilding can be seen in the building blocks of Venice, layer upon layer; the city lifting itself slowly out of the lagoon.

Despite the efforts of a thousand years of Venetian engineering, at the beginning of the twentieth century the vulnerability of the city remained all too real. When new pressures were brought to bear, the viability of the city was seriously called into question. The greatest of these pressures was the industrial development to the west, which involved intensive groundwater extraction, triggering the subsidence of the entire area, Venice included. This, combined with a long-established pattern of slow sea-level rise, meant that by the end of the century Venice was 23cm lower than in 1900 and there had been a tenfold rise in the frequency of tides higher than 110cm – the level at which the city begins to flood. On 4 November 1966 a high tide of 194cm caused catastrophic flooding in Venice, Chioggia and the other settlements of the lagoon. Although groundwater extraction was halted shortly after this flood, the threat of such exceptionally high tides remains and the lagoon has narrowly escaped similar disasters on several occasions since.

Venetians have coped as best they can. Doorways at canal level, where once residents alighted from boats and *gondole*, have been bricked up or turned into windows. Many lower floors have been abandoned altogether. Doors that open on to the narrow passageways that criss-cross the city are protected with flood guards when not in regular use. Temporary walkways are erected when the squares are drowned.

Unfortunately for modern Venetians, rebuilding at a higher level is no longer an option. A city that has replaced trade with tourism as its principal source of revenue cannot afford to tear down its neighbourhoods and build them afresh. Although there is an ongoing programme of raising quay-sides and renewing embankments there is a limit to how far a pavement can be raised if the doorway thresholds are staying put. This is why the oldest parts of the city, above all the Piazza San Marco,

Flooding is all too common an occurrence in St Mark's Square.

Few of the traditional doorways to Venetian homes are used today but, with a little adaptation, the rooms can still be lived in.

are the most frequently flooded, for they have been raised the least.

There are, however, a few corners of the city where radical redevelopment is still possible. The large island that defines the southern boundary of the city, the Giudecca, is home to several new housing developments fashioned out of the spaces, and in some instances the buildings, where industry once flourished. Where a Junghans watch factory used to stand there are now striking apartment blocks, colourful and playful in the manner of Venice but detailed with a wholly modern sensibility. As you approach the new district of Ex-Junghans along the narrow paths of the Giudecca a tell-tale clue of what lies ahead appears before you: steps. A short flight of steps marks the boundary with the new district, which has, as with every other rebuild in Venice before it, been raised a few more centimetres.

The Ex-Junghans district expresses the city's confidence in its future despite the problems it faces. The apartments are designed to be not only attractive and functional but also robust, boasting resilient lower floors for those exceptionally high tides. The increased threat is accommodated without a repudiation of that which matters most to Venice, the water itself. The urban form is consistent with the rest of the city: a network of pedestrian and aquatic routes, including new canals and new views of the lagoon. These new houses, rising out of the waters of the lagoon, demonstrate that even on the most vulnerable of coasts it is possible to design, build and thrive with confidence and optimism.

The Venetians do, however, have special cause for confidence. For, if all goes to plan, by 2012 the entire lagoon will be protected from dangerously high tides by the great gates of the MOSE Project. MOSE (Modulo Sperimentale Elettromeccanico) was conceived as the ultimate response to the city's vulnerability to high tides. If it is no longer possible to raise the city, the only alternative, other than abandonment, is to control the water that threatens it. After years of deliberation, the practical realisation of this alternative is a range of engineering interventions dominated by the construction of new barriers at each of the three inlets to the lagoon.

The Lido, Malamocco and Chioggia inlets are small relative to the length of the littoral islands that protect and define the lagoon, but are nonetheless extremely wide if you are an engineer planning to build movable barriers across them. The Lido inlet is 800m wide, the Malamocco inlet 400m wide and the Chioggia inlet 380m wide. The waters that flow through them are vital to maintaining the ecological health of the lagoon, and the boats that

Venetian day trippers to the Lido consider the size of the channel that will be protected by the barriers of the MOSE project.

This innocuous stairway indicates the boundary of the redeveloped southern quarters of the Giudecca. Whenever the city is rebuilt, it is raised.

New apartments on the Giudecca maintain the city's open relation to the water but incorporate flood-resilient ground floors.

navigate them are just as vital to maintaining the economy and way of life of the inhabitants. Therefore any barriers must be traversable in ordinary circumstances but strong and effective when high tides threaten. The solution is a row of hinged concrete gates with internal cavities that, under normal conditions, are filled with water and so lie upon the sea bed, keeping the waterways above clear. When high tide presents a risk to the lagoon, the gates are filled with compressed air and rise up to face the surge, holding a difference in height between sea and lagoon of up to two metres. Each gate moves under the pressure of the sea so that the structure as a whole is both flexible and robust. A total of 78 gates will span the three inlets to the lagoon.

MOSE includes many other elements other than the centrepiece gates. New breakwaters are being constructed outside the inlets to reduce the speed of the incoming tide, and the bed of the Malamocco inlet is being raised to reduce the volume of incoming water. A lock is also being built at the Malamocco inlet to allow the passage of shipping when the gates are closed. In addition, work is ongoing to protect the sea-facing beaches of the littoral islands, which are particularly vulnerable to storm surges from the Adriatic; to renew embankments throughout the lagoon; and to enhance the quality of the marine environment by reconstructing mudflats and salt marshes and decontaminating areas affected by industrial pollution.

The MOSE barriers will lie on the floor of the lagoon and be raised by compressed air when the sea threatens.

The MOSE Project was conceived as a necessary response to existing threats to the settlements of the lagoon. The designers did, however, recognise that the problem of sea-level rise is likely to get worse. Therefore the gates will be able to cope with a further 60cm rise, just beyond the 2007 IPCC projection of a 18-59cm sea-level rise this century. Inevitably, some feel that this is not precautionary enough, given the signs that climate change may be progressing faster than expected. Nonetheless, Venice will soon be one of the best-protected coastal cities in the world and will remain so for decades to come.

Venice will not last forever. No city in the world will last forever. But the inevitability of future decline is never a sufficient reason for writing off a settlement today. Whatever the threat may be, there are always options of defence and adaptation. The issue is whether the cost of such options is judged to be worthwhile, given the extra life that the settlement will gain. For Venice, this price is manifestly worth paying. It may be that in 200 years Venice will be inundated and abandoned, but this does not diminish the value of the city now and in the decades to come. If vulnerability is truly part of the magic of Venice, the long-term prospects of sea-level rise make the city of today and tomorrow only that bit more precious and worth defending.

The long retreat of England

In the south-east of England the gentle hills of the South Downs come to an abrupt and dramatic halt in the chalky cliffs of East Sussex and Kent – a great white incision between the sea and the sky. The natural theatre of this coast is just as awe-inspiring as the architectural fireworks of Venice, but here the unassuming tourist is more likely to be struck by the power and permanence of the landscape than by its vulnerability. The White Cliffs have always represented the fortress-like independence of England, a mighty stone set in a silver sea.

This permanence is, however, a chimera. For chalk is a soft rock that cannot stand forever against the power of the sea but crumbles and falls, spitting out pebbles and stones from ancient seas that are washed once more by the ocean and turn the beaches porcelain-blue. Little by little, the cliffs are worn away.

At the village of Birling Gap, just west of the famous cliffs of Beachy Head, the consequences of this erosion for coastal communities are all too evident. A terrace of cottages built for the coastguards stands at the top of the cliffs, simple and elegant with a symmetrical form accentuated by the green-painted finish on the middle cottage. The symmetry has, however, long gone, destroyed by the demolition of the two seaward cottages in the face of the slowly retreating cliff. The National Trust, which owns the cottages and the neighbouring hotel, has made clear that the entire settlement will in due time meet the same fate: "Our priority is for the coastline to evolve naturally and allow the undefended cliff to move".[6] Although this is the most extreme of a range of policy options currently being pursued by the Trust along the 608km of British coastline it owns, the strategic approach adopted for all its properties is to take a long-term view, working with natural coastal change wherever possible.

Coastguards' cottages at Birling Gap in East Sussex.

The impacts of climate change on sea levels, and potentially on the energy in the seas and the skies, are hard realities for landowners in the south-east of England to accept. On any given day, the landscape seems so strong and secure, despite the hurling wind and raging sea. Yet from the perspective of history, this landscape has always been changing, retreating slowly as the sea takes its toll. Immediately to the east of Birling Gap, traces of an ancient hill fort can still be seen: an embankment that once supported a rampart encircles the prominent hill where a lighthouse now stands. Yet the circle is now a semicircle and the hill has been cut away down its centre. The jagged teeth of the cliff edge are now bared where the central hall of the fort may once have stood.

Continue east along this coast and you soon come to a settlement with a much greater claim to protection than Birling Gap: the seaside resort of Eastbourne, which still boasts a traditional pier, carefully cultivated gardens and a promenade bordered with hotels offering afternoon tea. It is also home to 95,000 people. Eastbourne may not be Venice but there is too much at stake here to let the sea have its way. Here the beach is all-important, for it provides the primary line of defence for the town against the encroaching sea, as well as attracting the crowds in the summer sunshine. So the beach is artificially replenished to ensure that its defensive role is maintained: trucks regularly empty tonnes of gravel and sand between the wooden groynes that help to keep the beach in

place. For now, Eastbourne is going nowhere. In time, however, the sea will deepen the foreshore and slowly steepen the beach. Repair and restoration will become ever more difficult and, at some point in the decades or centuries to come, this meticulously protected coastline will eventually give way.

These tensions between acceptance of the inevitability of change and the will to protect and preserve are even more pronounced on England's most vulnerable coastline, East Anglia. For here there are dozens of coastal towns and villages that are not big enough or important enough to be confident of long-term protection but that are nonetheless valued places and communities. There are medieval villages, Norman churches and beautiful manor houses. There are oldcomers and newcomers; thousands of people for whom this coastline is their home.

The coast of East Anglia is vulnerable both to the steady eroding power of the tide, which cuts at the foundations of the sand and clay cliffs, and to the destructive power of storm surges from the North Sea. If such a surge, driving high waters towards the narrow strait of the English Channel, combines with a high tide, when the moon and the sun are in alignment, the force of the sea on the exposed coast can be devastating.

Over the centuries the coastline of East Anglia has given up dozens of villages, hundreds of homes

Left: The lighthouse at Birling Gap stands atop the remnants of a hill where an ancient fort once stood, encircled by a defensive embankment.
Right: Renewing the beaches of Eastbourne.

and thousands of acres of farmland to the sea. Given the speed with which any coastline gains an impression of permanence, this history is easy to forget, though every now and then this past catches coastal inhabitants and visitors by surprise. On 9 August 1888 the pleasure craft *Victoria* set sail from Cromer on the Norfolk coast, taking its passengers back to Yarmouth to complete their seaside day trip. The weather was fine and the sea was calm but shortly out of harbour the boat ran aground and was holed. It transpired that the boat had struck the top of the tower of the church of Shipden, a once-thriving village east of Cromer that had disappeared beneath the waves. All the passengers were rescued but the boat eventually sank and the area became known to mariners as Church Rock. This was the last vestige of a village that had once supported a population of over a hundred and maintained a prosperous harbour.

Similar stories can be told of villages all along the Norfolk coastline. Newton Cross once lay beyond the village of Hopton, which now fronts the sea. East of Winterton, the village of Ness once stood on a headland where a lighthouse was maintained; village, headland and lighthouse have now all disappeared. Great Waxham was once paired with Little Waxham but the little sibling is no more. Seaward of Happisburgh, the village of Whimpwell boasted a manor inhabited by the Abbot of St Benet; now Happisburgh itself is falling into the sea. As at Shipden, the church of the ancient village of Eccles was the last building to go; the tower standing mournfully on the beach until it was finally toppled by a storm in 1895.[7]

The modern residents of the Norfolk coast are ambivalent about this history. In the words of one local activist, "we can't hold back Mother Nature, but we can make it tough for her".[8] This was effectively government policy in much of the latter half of the twentieth century, when substantial defences were built to protect the coastal communities of East Anglia – a policy in part driven by the experience of the devastating 1953 floods when thousands lost their lives. In some vulnerable areas, concrete sea walls were built. Elsewhere, beaches were protected by wooden revetments and, latterly, mounds of Scandinavian granite

Left: The cliff-top village of Happisburgh, Norfolk, viewed through neglected and ineffective defences.
Right: The church tower of the lost village of Eccles, prior to its reclamation by the sea.

boulders. By the end of the century, when all these defences were beginning to show their age, public policy had changed its tune. The idea that it is possible with modern engineering to 'hold the line' in perpetuity has been discredited. Although some stretches of the coastline will continue to be protected, at least for the next 50 years, many others will not. Adaptation and 'risk management' are now the dominant themes of coastal erosion policy.[9]

In part, the problem lies with the defences themselves. As is so often the case when we try to make the environment do our bidding, interventions designed for one purpose end up producing all sorts of unintended consequences. A sea wall may protect the land immediately behind it but it also has the effect of exposing the unprotected beaches on either side to greater erosion. Over time, as these beaches recede, the protected land becomes a promontory and so becomes vulnerable to being outflanked by the sea unless further leeward defences are built. Any beaches immediately in front of the sea wall disappear as the foreshore is progressively deepened by the force of the waves. Such promontories also prevent the neighbouring beaches from being recharged with sand or shingle from further along the coast – a process that is vital to the maintenance of the beaches and their function as a natural defence. As sea levels rise, the increasingly fragile beaches are themselves slowly decimated.

In contrast, the natural erosion of the coastline turns out to be self-limiting. As cliffs are eroded, the resulting sediment is washed along the coastline and builds the beaches and dunes that control the erosion even if they don't stop it. The bigger and broader the beach, the more effective the defence. Break this system down with artificial defences (which, unlike those in Venice, stay permanently up) and you risk forfeiting your invaluable natural defences and everything that goes with them – including sandcastles, tourists and wildlife. It is this analysis that has led to 'managed realignment' gaining greater priority in shoreline policy.[10] It may be that the best defences for exposed coastal communities are not barriers and blocks but artificial sandbanks beyond the shoreline that add to the natural defences rather than disrupt them.[11]

The future is bleak for villages such as Happisburgh, despite the determined efforts of their residents to protect their history, property and community. Unlike the more substantial resort of Cromer, which will continue to be protected at least in the medium term, Happisburgh and similar cliff-top villages have been told that policy in the short, medium and long term is to "allow retreat through no active intervention".[12] By the middle of this century, if erosion proceeds as anticipated, Happisburgh's twelfth-century church of St Mary's will be teetering on the edge of the cliff, preparing to meet the fate of so many Norfolk churches before it.

Unless, that is, action is taken to preserve the church before the fatal hour. When the cliffs crept too close to the ancient parish church of Sidestrand, the local people decided that the only way to protect their long-established place of worship was to move it. A final service was held in the church on Christmas Day 1880 before the entire building, bar the tower, was moved stone by stone a third of a mile inland. A year later, with a new tower, the villagers celebrated another Christmas within its rebuilt walls.

Historically, relocation has always been the primary human response to coastal erosion. Over the last 200 years this fact has been buried under the substantial sea defences that have made possible a much more extensive development of the coast than could ever be achieved before. But the limitations of these defences are now becoming clear. In the long term, relocation may be the only option even for the better-protected towns of Norfolk. As their concrete sea walls turn the towns into artificial headlands, jutting out from a receding coastline, the defences themselves will become increasingly difficult to maintain. As the waters beyond them deepen and the size and power of the waves increases, effective defence will become ever more difficult and expensive.[13]

Concrete defences stand firm today but will be of little value when the beaches before them are scoured and swept away.

The beach huts that valiantly face the waves on their concrete battlements will be easy to move, but the brick-and-block dwellings behind them will not. Beaches have long been places for curious English rituals, but we will have to find new rituals for giving up our cherished homes to the power of the sea.

Venice-on-Thames

In England, as in Italy, some settlements are considered to be worthy of greater protection than others. So while the villages of Norfolk fall into the increasingly turbulent seas, the metropolis of London will be defended from the rising tide for many years to come. Whether the city's defences will cope in practice with the ever-increasing pressures upon them is, however, another matter.

London has some of the best tidal defences in the world. The Thames Barrier, opened in 1984, is the city's principal line of defence against tidal surges from the Thames estuary. It is the most prominent part of an extensive network of defences that work together to ensure that when the Barrier is closed flooding does not occur elsewhere. The Thames Tidal Defences include 185 miles of flood walls, 35 major gates and over 400 minor gates.

Severe tidal surges in the Thames estuary are unusual but very dangerous. They occur when a deep Atlantic depression moves south-east down the North Sea to the English Channel, driving excess water into a very confined space. When exacerbated by a high incoming spring tide and strong winds, water levels can be three metres higher than normal. As well as protecting the city from this threat, the Thames Barrier also helps to reduce the risk from the river itself. If heavy rainfall swells the Thames and its tributaries to dangerous levels, the Barrier can be closed to shut out the tide and so provide more capacity for the river.

The Thames Barrier, the heart of the Thames tidal defences.

All the forces that contribute to flood risk in London are likely to worsen over this century. Sea levels will rise, winter rains will be heavier and storms may become more frequent. The post-glacial sinking of the south-east of England will also continue unabated. Even in the two decades since the Thames Barrier opened, the frequency of closures has increased significantly. In 2000 the Barrier closed 24 times, more than in the first ten years of operation combined.

Despite these increasing hazards, there are currently no plans to build a new barrier. According to the Thames Estuary 2100 Project, this is likely to be necessary only if peak tide levels increase by more than three metres. For less extreme scenarios, other options are available. These include improving existing defences, moving some defences and creating more space for water by using open land downstream of the Barrier to hold tidal flood water – recreating the long-compromised Thames floodplain (see pages 66-8).

One day, however, the defences will be breached, and it might be prudent to start planning for that day sooner rather than later. Unlike the Venetians, who are building their barrier in response to the experience of inundation, Londoners have successfully kept the waters at bay. Consequently, London has an infrastructure that despises water. Venice has canals and *vaporetti* (water buses); London has

Little Venice, Kensington, London. A model for London in 2100?

underground tunnels and electric trains. The inundation of large areas of London, especially densely populated boroughs immediately south of the river, may seem unthinkable today. But never let a crisis go to waste.[14] If there does come a time when the defence of London, like the defence of Norfolk, can no longer be sustained, it may be possible to carve out a city with a new and productive relationship with the river and the sea. London has not always despised the water. The city does, after all, owe its existence to the Thames, the great eighteenth-century highway that took the king to Hampton Court and his ambassadors to the English Channel. In the nineteenth century, the Grand Union Canal further transformed the aquatic transport infrastructure, connecting the centre of the city to the industry of the North. In living memory, the port of London was a thriving hub of world trade. Today, the Grand Union Canal still winds its way into the heart of the city through the well-to-do boroughs of Camden, Islington and Kensington, though its coal barges have long been replaced by pleasure boats. Flanked by elegant Regency and Victorian villas, the canal comes to an end in a basin where highly desirable waterside properties sell for millions. Perhaps, if Venice-on-Thames is the long-term future for London,[15] the charming streets of Little Venice are a reminder that, when this future is upon us, all need not be lost.[16]

Chapter six
Storms

Climate change projections for the UK

Over the last 50 years, the incidence of severe storms in Britain has increased, especially in the south.[1] The great storm of 1987, which devastated the south of England, may have been an unusually prominent expression of a growing trend towards greater storminess. Some have concluded, on the basis of substantial evidence, that climate change is driving this change and that we face both a higher incidence of severe winter storms and higher wind speeds in the years ahead.[2]

Unfortunately, however, changes in storms and wind speeds have proved to be extremely difficult to predict within climate models, not least because of the large natural variations in wind patterns. Some models do indicate significant increases in wind speeds in Britain (typically those that project an increase in the north–south pressure gradient across Europe[3]), but others do not. The Met Office's climate projections in 2002 included increases in winter wind speeds in the south and east of Britain of up to 10 per cent by the 2080s, with smaller increases elsewhere and wind-speed reductions in the summer in most areas.[4] But by 2009, when new climate projections for the UK were published, the Met Office had given up on making such predictions. The range of results from climate models concerning both the direction and strength of winter storms was so divergent that no confident conclusions could be drawn about what the future holds[5] (see Figure 6.1).

Further investigation of the incidence of storms in Britain over the twentieth century has also highlighted the difficulty of discerning clear trends, given the role that large-scale natural climate variability plays in shaping both the intensity and frequency of storms.[6] The 1980s and 1990s were stormy decades, but neither was as stormy as the 1920s.

This chapter does not, therefore, rest on the kind of solid scientific evidence enjoyed by the last four chapters. It is included in this book for three reasons. Firstly, the difficulty involved in modelling storms and wind speeds should not lead us to assume that all will be well. Secondly, if we accept the evidence that the planet is heating up, we might reasonably expect the extra energy in the climate system to produce some surprises. There is certainly evidence internationally that the planet's climate is becoming more turbulent.[7] Thirdly, the cost of ignoring the issue could be immense.

The last of these points is critical: homes and settlements built today ought to be designed to cope with all the weather that we might reasonably expect the rest of the century to bring. If we are not sure what we face, the best we can do is to assess the risk and consider the cost of inaction. This is an argument based on the principles of risk management rather than climate science but, in the case of storms, it is persuasive: we should prepare for higher wind speeds and more intense storms precisely because the cost of these events would be extremely high, even though we do not have high confidence that they will happen. The insurance industry estimates the cost of a major storm in Britain to be around £1.5 billion.[8]

The principles of risk management already inform modern building standards, which are intended to reduce the risk of a building incurring costs due to poor performance once the builders have left. Since 1944, design wind load has been integral to these standards, which ought to mean that modern houses are better protected from high wind speeds than old houses, especially as the latter also suffer from the effects of long-term exposure to the elements, potentially leading to deterioration in the components that hold the building together and keep the roof on. In practice, this may not be the case, as builders can treat 'minimum standards' as targets and use materials and methods of construction that are not as robust as those of traditional building. There is evidence that many modern homes are in fact more vulnerable to storms than older homes, which were genuinely built to last.[9]

The impact of increasing wind speeds can be estimated using historical data on wind damage.

Table 6.1 is drawn from four decades of wind-damage records and shows how the expected number of damaged houses is likely to rise if wind speed increases. Although the estimates in Table 6.1 are less reliable for higher wind speeds, they match historical experience. For example, in the great storm of 1987, when maximum wind speeds were up to 7 per cent higher than design values, 1.3 million houses were damaged.

To some, a risk-based approach to planning for the future may seem overly cautious. If nothing else,

however, it is rational. In principle, it avoids the need to actually make a judgement about whether an event will or will not happen. Consequently, the approach has been used successfully to advance the case for climate change mitigation strategies in the face of scepticism about the science. It may have just as important a role to play in advancing the case for adaptation, not least within a highly cost-conscious building industry.

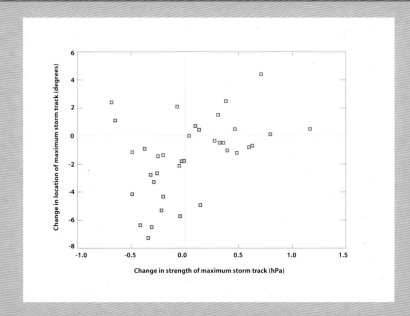

Figure 6.1. Change in location (degrees latitude) and strength (hPa) of maximum storm track over the UK for winters in the 2080s (from the 1961-1990 average) under a medium-emissions scenario.[10] © UK Climate Projections 2009. The red squares are from the UK Hadley Centre climate models; the blue squares are from other international climate models. Most of the international models suggest that the UK is going to get stormier in the years ahead, but most of the Hadley Centre models suggest the contrary.

Table 6.1. Expected number of damaged houses per storm in the UK as wind speed increases over the design wind speed required by the 1997 building code.[11]

Wind-damaged houses	Increase in wind speed					
	2 per cent	4 per cent	6 per cent	8 per cent	10 per cent	15 per cent
Max	634,000	817,000	1,054,000	1,347,000	1,705,000	3,077,000
Min	225,000	290,000	374,000	478,000	605,000	1,092,000

Facing the gale: the Western Isles

In the far north-west of Scotland, ancient mountain ranges face down the great weather systems of the north Atlantic. Ocean-saturated depressions are driven east by the jet stream and break over the glens, shrouding the landscape. As tourists and walkers know to their cost, wind and rain are facts of life in the Scottish Highlands.

The Western Isles, or Outer Hebrides, are the first line of defence against these storms, arcing 200 miles from Lewis in the north to Barra, the most southerly inhabited island. The mountains are lower here than on the mainland and fade away altogether in the long tail of the archipelago. The landscape of the Uists and Benbecula is characterised by heather-clad moors, scattered lochans and broad, luminous skies.

Here the wind races across the landscape unopposed, regularly reaching speeds of 80mph and more. The Western Isles get more sunshine than the mainland but the wind is relentless. Even on bright summer days the golden sands of Harris are chilled by the force of the Atlantic southwesterlies.

Although both the climate and the land can be unforgiving, farming communities have thrived on the Western Isles for millennia. The east coasts have the best of the limited shelter but the west coasts offer the most productive land, the machair, and it is here that many of the oldest settlements can be found. The remains of roundhouses from the early Iron Age nestle in the shelter of the dunes. Higher up, the Neolithic standing stones at Callanish speak of a continuity of civilisation across five thousand years.

The wind races across the low landscape of the Uists.

The traditional dwellings of the islands, commonly called 'black houses', evolved over the centuries in response to the demands of the people, the land and the climate. Although today most black houses lie in ruins, these seemingly simple buildings are exemplars of wind-resistant design. The subsistence farmers of the Western Isles may have led harsh lives by today's standards, spending much of their time outdoors on the moors and seas, but when they needed shelter from the storm they could turn to dwellings that were warm, dry and remarkably quiet.

Black houses were constructed of the materials to hand: rock, earth, wood, turf, heather and straw. Incredibly thick walls, typically constructed of two leaves of stone with a clay and earth fill between them, supported timber trusses and a roof of turf and oat-straw thatch. There was one door but no windows – just a small opening in the roof admitting light. Another small hole in the roof provided ventilation for the fire in the middle of the room below. The undivided interior was shared between livestock at one end, providing valuable heat in the winter, and the human residents at the other. Many black houses had an adjoining secondary chamber where animal feed could be stored. Although there were variations in the layout of the interior spaces across the different islands, the basic wind-resistant form was always the starting point.

The shape of the black house was incredibly aerodynamic: a long, low form, sitting deep in the landscape and pointing into the wind. The roof of the house looked a bit like an upturned boat, deflecting the wind as efficiently as a boat deflects water. The curved roof and corners kept the wind

The stones of Callanish, testament to five thousand years of civilisation on the Western Isles.

An aerodynamic form, a strong roof lashed down with boulders and few openings kept the interior of the black houses still, warm and quiet.

flowing round the building with minimum turbulence. Nothing protruded from the roof, and even wind-disruptive eaves were dispensed with: instead of protruding beyond the walls to shed water, the roof finished in the middle of the walls, the rain draining into the thick turf on top of the wall. As there were almost no openings the wind had few opportunities to get in and had no easy pathway through the inside of the building. The only significant opening, the door, was deeply recessed and often faced east, away from the wind.

The design was also exceptionally strong; the simple form allowing for a substantial construction. The thick stone walls were built up around the base of the roof trusses, so the low roof was anchored deep within the structure of the building. The roof timbers were pegged and lashed together and covered with the heavy turf and thatch layers. The thatch itself was kept in place with a net woven from heather rope, weighed down by a perimeter ring of tied-in boulders. The thick walls and roof protected and insulated the house, keeping rain, cold and noise out (in storm conditions the rain can be horizontal) and precious heat in. The fire was always kept burning in the central hearth space, its smoke escaping through the roof and enriching the turf as it went – every year a third of the thatch and soot-encrusted sods on the roof was replaced and the rich remains dug into the potato fields.[12] The room did not fill with smoke because, with no draughts despite the gale outside, the smoke rose from the fire undisturbed to the rafters.

Black houses served the isolated crofting communities of the Western Isles very well. These communities were largely self-sufficient and had little contact with the outside world, and these simple, strong houses built from local materials could be constructed and maintained without dependence on imported goods. Furthermore, the islanders had few expectations for their houses as they lived their daily lives predominantly in the open air. If the moor and the sky are the boundaries of your home, four stone walls and a roof are of secondary importance, a necessary shelter from the storm but not a focus for domestic ambition.

Everything was geared to the demands of subsistence: as well as providing shelter, the house contributed to the farming year by providing compost from the roof and manure from the interior byre.

The black house crofters were tenant farmers, and in the late eighteenth and nineteenth centuries their well-to-do landlords took an increasing interest in both their farming practice and the quality of the buildings they inhabited. Inspired by changes to agriculture in the Scottish lowlands, the landlords of the Western Isles sought to improve the productivity of their land while also improving conditions for their tenants, thereby demonstrating their own enlightenment as landlords. A particular focus of concern was the seemingly unhealthy practice of people and animals inhabiting the same space with minimal division between the two. Consequently, instructions were sent to tenants to introduce two doors, one for humans and one for cattle, and to partition the interior. Chimneys and windows were also promoted to improve interior conditions.[13]

To modern eyes such changes seem the most basic prerequisite for civilised living, yet they were fiercely resisted by the crofters, who were evidently very satisfied with the building design that had met the needs of their families for generations. Change came only when crofting society itself changed, especially when the isolation of the self-reliant communities began to diminish. New roads, seasonal employment on the Scottish mainland, the growth of local industry, public health education campaigns and involvement in foreign wars all helped to transform the expectations of the islanders. In the early twentieth century, partitions, windows, chimneys, fireplaces and even wallpaper all became common.

Ultimately, despite these changes, the buildings themselves were not considered appropriate for modern life. In the 1920s local authorities offered loans and grants to enable people to build 'white houses' (so called because of their rendered walls) made from concrete. By the 1960s most black houses functioned only as byres, the humans

A miniature rebuilt black house sits alongside the white house that replaced the original building on North Uist.

having moved to their new homes with electricity, sanitation, carpeted floors and square-cornered gables. The last black house residents moved out to occupy new council houses in 1974.

The white houses were compact and strong; they had small windows and sat low in the landscape. But their performance in the wind could not match the black houses. The windows rattled, draughts shot through the building and the roofs were vulnerable in high winds. The extraordinary still, quiet calm of the interior of the black house had been lost forever.

Never ignore the power of the storm

The black house was a product not only of a particular climate and geography but also of a particular culture and way of life. Its time has

passed. The wind, however, blows as furiously as ever. Storm resilience is just as critical to the design of houses in the Western Isles as it has always been, yet it is all-too-easily neglected as a design priority when there are so many other competing demands on the specification of modern homes. In the great storm of 2004, roofs, garages, extensions, conservatories and outbuildings tumbled across the landscape of the Western Isles, reminding local people of the cost of disregarding the force of the elements. Kit houses and pattern-book designs may be cheap, but they are unlikely to cope well with long-term exposure to north Atlantic gales.

Robust simplicity is undoubtedly the best starting point for wind-resistant design, whether of the black house or white house variety. Yet it is possible to build altogether more ostentatious dwellings and still survive the storm if every design detail is treated with due care. In Stornoway, the principal town of the Western Isles, there is an urban tradition of house building that demonstrates

The solid villas of Stornoway have strong roofs, protected roof edges, recessed windows and rendered walls.

how quite elaborate buildings can be adapted to cope with severe wind conditions. In the nineteenth century, when crofters were sticking fast to their byre-living rooms, the citizens of Stornoway were erecting imposing town houses, as grand as the Victorian villas of Glasgow and Edinburgh. These houses may not be aerodynamic but they are built of stone so they have no problem standing firm against the wind. The rebated doors and windows are protected from the direct force of the wind. The steep roofs prevent the wind from getting under the tiles, and the edges of the roofs, where tiles are often exposed, have substantial protective finishes. Under the tiles, you are likely to find a sarking board – in effect a wooden finish like floorboards, laid across the structure of the rafters to which the tiles are double-nailed. The walls are rendered to fend off the horizontal rain.

The port of Stornoway does, however, benefit from the natural shelter of the landscape. As you travel out of the town, tall mansions give way to low, ground-hugging boxes. Most modern houses in the Western Isles are variations on the white house: low, square and relatively simple. Such houses cope with the gales but have limited charm as modern living spaces. The small windows and compact interiors express the basic need for shelter but the landscape is shut out. This mattered little in the days of the black house, when so much of life was lived outside, but today lifestyles and expectations have changed and an inward-looking home seems a missed opportunity when the landscape at the door is so stunning.

It is, however, possible to have the best of both worlds: to exploit the principles of storm resistance that the black houses embody with the modern desire to connect living space and landscape. Many of the houses designed by Skye-based architects Dualchas Building Design achieve this balance with considerable flair. Although the aesthetic is modern, there is an obvious debt to the black houses in the form and

A low, compact form with small windows is robust in the wind but shuts out the landscape.

details of their simple but desirable homes. The form of the Shed on Skye is long and low, pointing into the wind. The roof has minimal protrusions and there are no eaves or external gutters. The materials are simple and robust: corrugated metal roofing and durable larch weatherboarding facing the horizontal rain. High levels of insulation keep the warmth in and the cold and noise of the gale out. At the same time the potential of the site, just above the shore on one of the most beautiful coastlines in the world, is fully exploited thanks to the generous picture windows that open the interior to the depth and breadth of the landscape. This wholly modern feature is possible because, when the gale rages, the expanse of glass can be protected by integral storm shutters which slide across the facade. Only then does the focus of the occupants turn inwards to the fireplace, in the manner of so many black house residents before them.

Many of the other houses designed by Dualchas demonstrate their debt to the old vernacular forms of the black houses. Even the secondary chamber

finds its way into their reinterpretation, transformed from byre to bedroom. By translating the wisdom of the black houses into a modern idiom, the designers successfully satisfy both the modern need for daylight and fabulous views and the ancient need for wind and storm protection.

Return to source

The black house has an even stronger hold on Stornoway-based architect Stuart Bagshaw, who has devoted his professional life to understanding the role that these ancient buildings played at the heart of crofting life in the Western Isles. Although he recognises the difficulties involved in returning to a building type that would never pass modern building regulations, he celebrates the form and the materials of the black houses in his earthen, hairy houses that all but merge into the landscape. Blue Reef villas in Harris are tucked into the hillside, their heavy stone walls, grass roofs and long, low forms evoking the texture as well as the shape of the black house. These, however, are holiday lets, not

Above & bottom left: The Shed by Dualchas Building Design. The form is inspired by the black house but the materials and engineering are modern. Storm shutters open to bring in the light when conditions are calm.

Bottom right: Blue Reef villas by architect Stuart Bagshaw are tucked into the hillside and evoke the materials as well as the form of the old black houses.

Black Sheep House in the south of Harris. Owners and self-builders Pete and Christine Hope enjoy the force of the wind on their deep turf roof.

The double-chambered form of the Arnol black house is the inspiration for this modern home by Dualchas Building Design. Their well-insulated buildings need little heat, but a wood-burning stove is invaluable in the depths of the Scottish winter.

byres, so picture windows follow the wind-facing curve that would once have been a stone wall.

On the south coast of Harris, Black Sheep House illustrates the same approach. Constructed on the ruins of an old black house, the walls were rebuilt with many of the original stones by owner and dry-stone-wall builder Pete Hope. When he and partner Christine put the turf roof on they felt they were 'rubbing out' the house, so effectively does it merge into the landscape. Like the villas at Blue Reef, the front of the house boasts a curved picture window and the only problem with the wind to date has been with this modern addition, since the wind has blown rain into the building from underneath the window frames. The turf roof is not only strong and aerodynamic, it is also highly durable and will cope, indeed flourish, with increasingly intense rainfall and sunshine alike – serious threats to the long-term performance of many ordinary roofing materials.

Balancing the needs of the client with the demands of the climate is the core challenge for architects and builders in all climates that

experience extremes. The problem was impeccably resolved by the builders of the black houses, but increasing wealth and expectations have made the task ever more difficult. Simple houses with many inhabitants have been replaced by complex houses with few inhabitants. Although there are adaptive solutions for most designs, from Victorian mansions to sleek contemporary homes, no modern design matches up to the simple, hand-built form of the black house, made from the materials of the earth and rebuilt by anyone willing to get their hands dirty.

What you can do

All houses are built to withstand specified wind loads. If you are building a new house or doing major renovations, ask your engineer or architect what wind loads he or she is designing to and consider raising them. Roof design is especially critical as it is roofs that bear the brunt of wind and turbulence.

The following design principles describe how wind loads on buildings can be minimised.[14] It is

Hedges and trees provide an excellent first line of defence against the wind.

striking how well these principles, derived from building engineering, match the evolutionary tradition of the black house builders.

- Align the strong axis of the structure into the prevailing wind direction.

- Minimise the height of vertical walls.

- Avoid large openings (or potential openings such as glazing) on windward walls.

- Use hip or mansard roofs instead of conventional duo-pitch and flat roofs.

- Minimise eaves overhangs.

- Avoid shallow mono-pitch roofs.

- Minimise the use of right-angled corners on eaves and walls.

- Where possible, arrange buildings in a way that maximises the benefits of shelter and avoids large variations in height between adjacent buildings.

The principles above concern the form of the building and its setting. The following points address the wider issues of materials, roof design, openings and shelter.

- Use heavy materials and tie structural elements down.

- Protect walls exposed to the prevailing wind and rain with robust finishes such as lime

If your site is windy, seek shelter in the landscape: low houses hug the hillside of Eriskay on the Western Isles. The building on the wind-blown hilltop is the church.

render, durable timber or stone. Maintain all exposed finishes.

- Do not fill cavity walls with insulation if they are likely to face wind-driven rain.

- Avoid dormers and roof windows.

- Use a sarking board between the roof timbers and the tiles (the felt goes between the sarking board and tiles). Double-nail the slates.

- Consider an intensive (deep) green roof if you have the structure to support it, as this will protect the primary roof coverings from the UV and weather damage that leads to their deterioration and vulnerability in storms.

- Minimise roof protrusions: install television aerials in the loft and remove unused chimneys.

- Set windows and doors back from the exterior wall line. Specify high-quality windows and doors to prevent driving rain penetrating the seals. Maintain all seals around windows and doors.

- Always ensure that every window is shut when the wind increases.

- Build into the landscape as far as possible and exploit natural shelter.

- Build or plant shelter screens.

Chapter seven
Energy security

The future of energy

On 23 July 2007 rising flood waters from the overtopped River Severn threatened to inundate an electricity substation at Walham in the county of Gloucestershire. Hundreds of houses in towns and villages across the county had already been overwhelmed by the flooding, which caused widespread havoc and distress, but serious damage to this obscure, unmanned switching station carried the risk of a much wider impact: the loss of power to half a million homes and to the government's intelligence-gathering centre. Following a high-level government meeting, a rapid operation was mounted to protect the substation, which had been built with no permanent flood walls. The entire site was encircled with temporary barriers, and high-powered mobile pumping units worked non-stop to remove the water that had already breached the site. The station was saved, but only just, for the waters had got to within two inches of the top of the temporary barriers.

Events such as this expose the vulnerability of modern energy supply to extreme weather events. We live in an energy-hungry world which is profoundly dependent on a complex national and international generation-and-distribution infra-structure. It is easy to take all of this for granted because, for most of us, the power stations, cables and gas pipelines are out of sight and out of mind. Yet modern society could not function without this secure supply of energy, most of which is still derived from fossil fuels. Our houses are heated and powered by them, our industry is driven by them and our cars, lorries, trains and planes are fuelled by them.

The threats to energy security from climate change are considerable. Storms regularly bring down power lines in Britain[1] and could cause mayhem across the national electricity grid if they get more severe and more frequent. Flooding threatens all parts of the energy infrastructure, including power stations, many of which are built on the coast. There are six huge power stations on the floodplains of the Thames and the Medway. Unlike the Walham switching station, they are built with good flood

defences but will nonetheless become increasingly vulnerable as weather events become more extreme. In North America heatwaves have triggered repeated breakdowns in electricity supplies because of overloading from air-conditioning systems.

Beyond these direct impacts of climate change, there are many more current and potential threats to Britain's energy security. In January 2009, the citizens of Bulgaria suffered a bitterly cold week without any heating in their homes because of a dispute between Ukraine and Russia over gas supplies – a crisis that made the European Union's dependence on Russian resources abundantly clear. After years of reliance on North Sea gas, Britain is now importing liquefied natural gas in tankers from the Middle East. The decline in North Sea oil is increasing the country's depend-ence on foreign suppliers from troubled regions: on current trends Britain will be importing four-fifths of its fuels by 2020.[2] Control of the international supplies of fossil fuels has long dominated global politics, explicitly or otherwise.

Then there is the problem of peak oil. Exactly when the world can expect the supply of oil and natural gas to peak and start to decline is hotly debated. The Organisation of Petroleum Export-ing Countries (OPEC) insists that there is plenty of oil to meet rising international demand for the next two decades at least and that "availability is not an issue".[3] Many independent experts disagree and some insist that we are already at the peak of oil supply.[4] The International Energy Authority (IEA), the most authoritative indepen-dent voice on the issue, claims that increased investment in existing fields, the discovery of new fields and the exploitation of non-traditional fuel sources such as the Canadian tar sands will keep the barrels rolling.[5] However, the IEA's chief economist has acknowledged that oil supplies are likely to plateau around 2020.[6]

Then there is the problem of Britain's electricity-generating capacity. With many coal-fired and nuclear plants due to be decommissioned in the next ten years, there is a real risk that the country will face regular 'brownouts' unless there is a rapid programme of new investment.[7] If we solve this problem by building more power stations driven by fossil fuels, we will only exacerbate the greater problem of climate change itself. If we are to address climate change and reduce global greenhouse gas emissions, we must rethink everything about how we produce and use energy.

Anyone building or renovating a house today has the opportunity to participate in this rethink. Every house built today should be designed for a life of at least a hundred years. Designers and planners ought therefore to be taking full account of a future of energy shortages and escalating fuel prices, just as they should take account of the direct impacts of climate change that are expected in this century. It will take time to wean a profligate world off fossil fuels, but every decision we make today should be a step towards this transformation.

Household energy supply is already a pressing concern for people on low incomes in hard-to-heat homes. In 2006, 3.5 million households in Britain needed to spend more than 10 per cent of their income on energy bills to stay warm – an increase on 2003 of 1.5 million households.[8] This increase was almost entirely due to increases in energy prices, triggered in part by constraints on supply. If people are suffering now because of high fuel prices, we need to redouble our efforts to make buildings and communities robust for a future of long-term price increases.

There is an obvious convergence between the demands of a world threatened by energy insecurity and the challenge of preventing runaway climate change. Both require a radical shift to a low-energy, low-carbon future. Without doubt, such a future will be our inheritance this century. The issue is simply how effectively and quickly we plan for it.

The hydro-electric plant on the Isle of Eigg in the Scottish Hebrides.

A community gets energised: the Isle of Eigg

If you catch a train from Glasgow and head north-west, the sprawling city and the urban lowlands rapidly give way to the more romantic landscape of Scotland: high mountain ranges, deep glens and bright, clean air. Much further north, this landscape becomes more brutal as the train heads across high open moors with no shelter from the storm, before descending once again to a coastline that becomes encrusted with silver beaches as the train nears its final stop, the port of Mallaig. From these beaches you can look out to the distant peaks of the Cuillins, the fearsome mountains at the heart of the Isle of Skye; or to the hulking shapes of the Small Isles, the scattering of islands south of Skye that rejoice in the names of Rhum, Eigg, Muck, Canna and Sanday.

The island of Eigg is the most easterly of the Small Isles and the second-biggest island after Rhum. Its name derives from the Norse for 'notch', presumably because there is a sizeable notch bitten out of its north-west coast. The beaches of Eigg have their own claim to fame: skirting the Singing Sands in the north are some of the most remarkable geological formations in the world, a 1960s sci-fi fantasy carved out of volcanic rock. In the south of the island, the local geology climaxes in the vertiginous Sgurr, an imposing but accessible mountain that provides a perfect walkers' viewpoint of the entire island.

Although Eigg has been inhabited for centuries, the population has ebbed and flowed with the troubled history of the Scottish Highlands. Below the high moors there are swathes of fertile farmland that reach down to sheltered bays, offering enough land to sustain a population of several hundred, although today there are only 86 permanent residents. Until the very end of the twentieth century the history of the island and the experience of its inhabitants had always been dominated by the power and interests of the island's landlord. Once these landlords had been clan chiefs (the Clan Ranald settled on Eigg), but latterly they were more likely to be rich businessmen, often with little interest in the well-being of their

The Isle of Eigg in the Scottish Hebrides.

tenants. Then, in 1997, after a long and protracted battle, the tenants of Eigg did the unthinkable and bought the island.

The resident buy-out of Eigg was a milestone in the history of the Highlands. It drew considerable national and international attention and has inspired other communities, with the support of the Scottish Government, to beat the same path. Freed from the unpredictable whims of a troublesome landlord, the residents of Eigg could at last focus their energies on improving their lot and building a flourishing, sustainable community. Very near the top of their new 'to do' list was the vital issue of energy.

Eigg is near enough to the mainland to dispel any feeling of remoteness, but far enough away to deny the islanders some of the key benefits of the modern world. Above all, Eigg has never been connected to the national grid, as laying an electric cable to the mainland would be prohibitively expensive. Consequently electricity remained a dirty and noisy business: the night air was filled with the sound of backyard generators, fuelled by diesel brought in on the ferry. This intimate relationship with power generation may have encouraged the islanders to be frugal and attentive to their energy use, but the sacrifice in their quality of life was all too evident. The magic of a secure supply of invisible power in the wall, something everyone on the mainland takes for granted, remained out of reach.

In the early days of their independence from their feudal overlords, many islanders wanted to resurrect the idea of laying a cable to the mainland, as this appeared to offer the only way of achieving a secure energy supply. Others, however, realised that there was an alternative on their doorstep. Why import electricity generated in distant power stations, fuelled by gas from under the North Sea (or much further afield), when you could open the front door and behold an environment endowed with a surfeit of renewable energy resources? On the west coast of Scotland, Eigg is not short of wind – and the wind brings rain, which soaks into the mountains that

Small farms occupy the fertile land between the high moors and the sea.

rise to 400 metres. Even the sun is surprisingly benevolent to the islanders.

Renewable energy was not unknown on the island in 1997. A handful of households had installed micro hydro systems, tapping into the power of the streams that flowed through their back gardens. These were acknowledged to be far superior to diesel generators as they quietly got on with the job of producing electricity without the need for regular fuelling. Only during prolonged dry spells did the back-up generators have to be switched back on. However, scaling up this experience to the entire island was simply not possible; there were not enough streams, near enough to everyone's homes, to make this viable. For everyone on Eigg to enjoy a secure energy supply without a cable to the mainland, something altogether more ambitious was needed: a new island electricity grid driven by a combination of natural energy resources.

Top: The hydro-electric plant provides the lion's share of the island's electricity needs.

Above left: Photovoltaic panels in perfect sunny conditions.

Above right: Four wind turbines face the imposing Sgurr.

The integration of the generation technology requires a room full of inverters and another full of batteries. John Booth, 'Mr Eigg Electric', looks on.

So a plan was hatched, a feasibility study conducted, a master plan produced and any remaining doubts among residents dispelled. From very early on, the idea of creating an electricity grid supplied by renewable energy captured the imagination of the islanders and gained 100-per-cent community backing. The details inevitably took a long time to work out. Unlike that of a traditional power station, the output of renewable energy generators cannot be controlled in response to demand. Renewable energy technologies are governed by the gods; all we can do is make the very best of what the gods choose to provide. In practice, this means both combining different types of energy-generation technology in the one system, in order to reduce the impact of the fluctuations in output from any one technology, and controlling demand to minimise peaks that may be difficult to meet.

After much deliberation and financial wrangling, the renewable-energy solution built on Eigg combines a 100kW hydro plant, four 6kW wind turbines and 10kW of photovoltaic panels. The dominance of the hydro-electric plant makes sense as this is the least intermittent of the three energy sources: the sun goes down every night and the wind drops but the rivers continue to flow long after it has stopped raining. However, even the west coast of Scotland has its dry spells, when the flow of water in the rivers falls below what is needed to run the hydro plant. Then, when the sun sets on still days, the system is forced to turn to the fourth element of power technology, the back-up diesel generator. The whole system is designed to provide 95 per cent of electricity from renewable resources on the island, with only the last 5 per cent coming from fossil fuels.

As well as producing a secure supply of electricity, the developers of the system also had to work out how to control and distribute the power across the island. The control of a collection of unpredictable and highly variable power sources to deliver a consistent output is far from easy and requires, on Eigg, two sheds full of technology, sited in the centre of the island. One shed contains a row of

inverters that turn the DC inputs from the power sources into a steady 240V AC output. The other is packed with batteries that absorb excess electricity, when output is greater than demand, and top up the supply when demand is greater than output. The supply of power across the island has unavoidably meant digging up all the roads (not that there are many) and laying a network of cables to all homes and businesses. The cabling of the island proved to be the most expensive feature of the entire project.

The island was 'switched on' on 1 February 2008. For the first time, everyone on Eigg had access to a secure supply of magic in the wall for 24 hours a day. The backyard generators were switched off and the welcome sound of silence filled the winter air. The new renewable energy supply was cheaper than the cans of diesel, and the money raised stayed on the island, paying for the system's new maintenance staff. Everyone was completely delighted.

The inhabitants of Eigg do not, however, have the liberty to burn power in the manner of their national-grid-connected neighbours on the mainland as there is a limit to how much the system can supply at any one time. In order to reduce peaks in demand, islanders are encouraged to spread their electricity use across the day rather than turning everything on at once. Every household has a 5kW cap on its power consumption and, if this is exceeded, the power cuts out. The cap for businesses is 10kW. Furthermore, every household has a live energy display meter which provides a constantly updated reading of how much power is being used and how much money is being spent within the house. This gives people an insight into their power consumption and helps them to work out the best ways of keeping their consumption down, stimulated by vigorous neighbourhood rivalry. Low-energy light bulbs and appliances are widely used.

These measures are important because energy conservation and energy efficiency are just as crucial to energy security as reliable supply. The less energy you need, the less pressure you put on the supply and the less of a problem you face when the energy cuts out. However, in the unusual setting of Eigg, where the transition has been not from profligacy but from frugal management of backyard generators, the new regime has inevitably led to some increases in energy use. Washing machines have arrived on the island for the first time. The stereo can be turned on at any time of day. Security of supply has meant that everyone can relax a little and enjoy life a little more.

Electricity is the most important aspect of energy security because we rely on electricity for so many things in the modern world. Yet we use far more energy to heat our homes than we do to power them. This point has not been lost on the people of Eigg, who are now exploring how they can ditch their reliance on imported coal and bottled gas in favour of locally sourced timber and solar-heated water, together with improvements in the energy efficiency of their buildings.

Wood is an excellent renewable resource as long as it comes from a well-managed forest where the trees are genuinely renewed. As there is already substantial forestry on Eigg, the islanders are in an excellent position to develop their plans for a woodland management scheme that will provide regular supplies of wood fuel to the community. Combining wood fuel and solar hot-water panels makes good sense: in the winter the wood provides both heating and hot water and in the summer the solar panels provide hot water when there is no need to burn wood for heating.

Energy dependence does not, of course, stop at the front door. The islanders are also planning to reduce the diesel burnt in vehicle engines on the island by replacing their old post van with a solar-powered electric van, creating a new public minibus service run in part on chip fat, and providing financial incentives for cycling. A new domestic recycling programme will also reduce

Maggie Fyffe, chair of the Eigg Trust, shows off the hand-held meter that keeps her informed of how much electricity she is using.

the number of times the waste lorry has to come to the island. In the longer term there are plans for high-efficiency wood boilers, solar porches, an anaerobic digester (to compost organic waste) and even a water taxi fuelled with renewable energy. The final piece of the jigsaw is the most challenging: the ferry. The people of Eigg still rely on the diesel-powered ferry for most of their supplies, for the tourist trade and for vehicle movements between the island and the mainland. Their relative isolation from the mainland may have provided the incentive to create their ground-breaking renewable electricity grid but it also constrains their potential for full energy autonomy. Nonetheless, as oil prices rise and the ferry becomes increasingly expensive, it is possible to imagine the people of Eigg surviving and thriving as ever more strategies for local energy independence are devised. They are clearly well ahead of the game.

The off-grid tradition

Back on the mainland, the energy obsessions of the people of Eigg all too easily disappear over the horizon. When security of energy supply is managed nationally, individuals and communities can forget all about it as long as they can afford to pay their bills. There are, however, many households on the mainland where interest in energy generation and consumption is as keenly felt as it is on Eigg – households which also have no connection to the national grid. One estimate puts the number of off-grid households in Britain at 25,000, although this includes people living in mobile homes, boats, vans and caravans.[9] Although for many static households the solution to off-grid living is simply to install a diesel generator and an oil-fired heating system, more imaginative and sustainable solutions can be found. Off-grid self-builders have long been pioneers of renewable energy.

The two households illustrated here are both the creations of people with deep commitments to local and global ecology. Tony Wrench's round-house in Wales is perhaps the fullest possible expression of off-grid living. It is built from timber, earth and straw sourced from the immediate environment. Its green roof is so abundant that the house all but disappears from view. The low energy needs of the household are supplied by a collection of renewable technologies on site: solar panels, a wind turbine and a wood burner. The owners, Tony and Faith, live simple, frugal and rewarding lives, giving as much back to the biosphere as they take from it.

The roundhouse 'hurts nothing or no one'[10] but has nonetheless been highly controversial. For Tony is keen not only to dramatically reduce his contribution to climate change but also to pursue a model of building and living that does not sit easily with a legal and planning history that denies ordinary people access to the land and opportunities to pursue radically low-impact lifestyles. The house was originally built without planning permission in defiance of this history but, thanks to its beauty and radicalism, has survived. At a time when we need as many exemplars of resilient design as possible, the destruction of this remarkable home would truly be a crime.

Nigel and Karen Lowthrop also live in a striking off-grid home, hidden within an ancient woodland. Hill Holt Wood is, however, much more than an attractive backdrop for an unusual home; it is also the setting for a flourishing social enterprise employing over twenty people, which integrates the management of the woodland and its resources with vocational training for unemployed and excluded young people. The whole project is designed to operate off-grid, incorporating appropriate buildings and renewable energy technology as part of a wider goal of managing the land, and the resources of the land, sustainably. The project makes the value of natural resources transparent to people who would otherwise be totally blind to them, and seeks to transform their lives in the process. Nigel and Karen's home, seemingly floating on a still pond in the enfolding forest, exemplifies the off-grid dream. Almost all of the energy needs of the household are met from natural resources available on site, using a solar hot-water

Top: Tony Wrench's self-built roundhouse, off-grid in every way.

Bottom: Nigel and Karen Lowthrop's delightful off-grid home, deep in the forest.

panel, solar photovoltaic panel, micro wind turbine and a wood stove. The only exception is cooking, which uses old-fashioned propane gas, though Nigel has plans for a biogas digester.

It is fitting that both these households are off-grid, for both express an independent spirit, a determination to see beyond the easy assumptions of the modern world and imagine ways of being, as individuals and as communities, that are appropriate for a troubled future. We should not, however, take this metaphor too literally and conclude that off-grid living is a model for all. For the national grid is itself an invaluable resource that is well worth keeping.

On-grid, low energy

The success of the renewable energy strategy on Eigg was wholly dependent on the creation of a new electricity network linking up all properties to the sources of generation. Although the island itself is 'off-grid', this local grid was needed to make the most of the available renewable energy by integrating inputs from different technologies, which tend to provide power at different times, and providing common back-up. Furthermore, even if there was a roof-top wind turbine on every dwelling, they would never have generated as much energy collectively as the four towering

These houses by Bill Dunster architects' ZEDfactory boast wind turbines and solar panels on their roofs, but what makes them really special is their exceptionally low energy demand.

turbines on the hillside. For wind at least, bigger systems produce much bigger results.

Over on the mainland, the national grid is just as critical to national renewable energy strategy. The grid integrates the outputs from intermittent technologies, provides back-up when needed and enables the development of larger systems at community or national level that can supply many homes at a lower cost per household than can domestic systems. Nationally, the provision of enough back-up capacity for renewable technology is a challenge without reliance on coal or nuclear power stations but it is possible, especially if a

good mix of renewable inputs is complemented by control of peak loads, as on Eigg. In the long term, the grid could offer distributed power storage as well as supply: if every vehicle was electric, the sheer number of stationary vehicles (i.e. batteries) connected to the grid at any moment might be enough, alongside existing storage methods, to do the job.[11]

Interconnectedness is a strength but it can also be a weakness. The shared benefits of a common system become shared problems when the system goes down. This is true not only of the electricity grid but also of the gas supply network and the

Top left: Russell Smith in front of the high-energy brick house that he has transformed into a low-energy home.

Clockwise from top centre: Interior insulation keeps the heat demand right down. The window reveals indicate the depth of what has been added. A hot-water panel and low-energy lights help to keep energy costs low.

Grove Cottage, before and after its radical ecorenovation. The thermal image illustrates just how little energy the renovated house loses compared with its neighbours. © Thermal Inspections Ltd 2009.

domestic oil-distribution network, all of which are likely to become more vulnerable to failure as the century progresses. A shift to renewable power and heat combined with major reductions in demand will make energy supply networks less vulnerable to the vagaries of international fossil-fuel markets, but any form of physical infrastructure will remain vulnerable to extreme weather.

Living in an on-grid home when the grid fails is not, however, a disaster if the home itself is designed to need very little energy to maintain a comfortable living environment. This is the hidden benefit of the many designs of Bill Dunster architects' ZEDfactory: although their homes are visually distinguished by renewable technology, it is the buildings' radically reduced energy demand that distinguishes their performance. In Northampton, a terrace of ZEDfactory homes uses power generated by the solar panels and wind turbines on the roof to drive heat pumps that pump solar energy absorbed in the ground under the houses to heat the interiors. If the wind drops at night, the heat pumps continue because the houses are grid-connected. If the grid fails, the residents can remain comfortably at home in the knowledge that the exceptional levels of insulation and draught-proofing will keep the heat in and prevent the houses rapidly cooling down.

Any house can be made robust in this way, though renovations of old, high-energy-consumption houses present all sorts of challenges once you go beyond the standard measures of insulating the loft and floors and draught-proofing the doors and windows. In Carshalton, South London, Russell Smith made it a personal mission to convert his cold Victorian end-of-terrace house into an exemplary low-energy renovation. The biggest challenge was the exterior walls, which were no more than a brick deep and in the winter shed heat with abandon. As he did not want to mess up the attractive exterior of the building, Russell doubled up the walls with insulation on the inside, building completely new interior wall finishes. Although this lost some space within the rooms themselves, the reward is a remarkably warm house with minimal heating bills.

The best way to keep heat inside an old building is, however, to add a new layer of insulation to the outside – a tea cosy that covers up everything, including the joins and junctions in the fabric of the building that remain a problem when internal insulation is installed. The renovation of a Victorian railway cottage near Hereford by Simmonds Mills Architects shows just how effective this approach can be when undertaken with a keen eye for every energy-conserving detail. Like so many Victorian homes, the original cottage had thin brick walls and was draughty and cold. The renovation was inspired by the ideas and experience of the Passiv-Haus movement in Germany, which promotes exceptional standards of building energy performance: the aim was to reduce the annual heat demand by up to 85 per cent. The renovated building stands proud of its original building lines thanks to its expanded roof and walls, grown fat with insulation. Viewed with a thermal imaging camera, the cottage glows blue in a line of bright yellow buildings – almost no heat escaping its solid, clean-cut form.

The radical reductions in energy demand achieved by these homes have multiple benefits beyond comfortable interiors and low costs. Firstly, low energy means low carbon emissions – zero in the case of renewably powered ZEDfactory homes – so the residents who live in these homes can do so in the knowledge that they are not adding to the burden of climate change. Secondly, any reduction in demand for energy improves collective energy security, for the less we need, the less vulnerable we are to problems with supply. Thirdly, although a future energy infrastructure supplied by genuinely renewable resources would remove many of the looming supply risks, such an infrastructure will be possible only if overall demand for energy is radically reduced. Renewable energy currently supplies only 2 per cent of Britain's primary energy,[12] and time is short. Finally, a low-energy home will always be the best place to be, other than an off-grid home, when the energy infrastructure fails.

As the era of cheap and plentiful fossil fuels draws to a close, everyone will have to learn to live with a good deal less energy. Our lives will change in myriad ways. Yet our homes can be just as comfortable and just as delightful as they are now, if not more so. There may be times when we have to go without, but with good design we will cope. Approached with the right frame of mind, less can almost always be more.

What you can do

If the power cuts out tonight or the gas supply fails or your oil runs out, how well will you cope? Houses that are designed to require very little energy are likely to be the most comfortable places to be when the energy supply fails. So before you think about installing your own private energy supply, renewable or otherwise, consider what you can do to make your home more resilient.

Begin by doing everything you can to keep the heat in and the cold out, as follows.

- Insulate your roof or loft. If you already have some loft insulation, it probably isn't enough – a foot thick is the recommended minimum now. If you want to use your loft for storage, pack soft insulation between the joists then put boards of solid insulation across them to create a surface.

- Insulate your walls. If you have cavity walls, get the cavity filled with insulation unless the wall is regularly exposed to driving rain. If you have solid walls, get quotes for exterior insulation (expensive but very effective) and interior insulation (less trouble but you lose some interior space).

- Insulate your ground floor. If you have a suspended timber floor, take up the floor, tack netting to the bottom of the joists and pack insulation between them. Solid floors can be insulated but this involves raising the floor level.

- Fix your windows. If you have old, draughty windows consider having them renovated (ensuring that this is done with draught-prevention as a priority) or replaced. Secondary glazing may be a cheaper option than full replacement.

- Draught-strip your doors, windows, keyholes and letterbox. Cover up exposed floorboards or fill the gaps between them with silicone. Use silicone to fill the gaps at the top and bottom of skirting boards.

Consider the following ways of reducing your dependency on electricity.

- Use a larder. Banished from modern houses thanks to the triumph of fridges, a small cool room does the job for most foodstuffs.

- Use daylight. If there are dark spots in your home where lights are often on during the day, consider installing roof windows or light tubes which channel light from your roof to a room below. Light-coloured walls, floors and ceilings help to bring daylight deep into rooms.

- If your house is vulnerable to overheating and you currently rely on air-conditioning, use every trick in the book to cool your house passively (see pages 45-6).

If you are keen to generate your own energy from local, renewable resources, much will depend on where you live and what resources are available.

- Wood is an excellent heat source if you live near a reliable supply. Enclosed wood burners are much more efficient than open fires.

- The sun can provide electricity, hot water and even limited space heating. All you need is an unshaded roof facing somewhere between south-east and south-west. Photovoltaic panels make electricity; solar thermal panels make hot water.

- The wind will generate electricity if it is unobstructed. Micro wind turbines are not much use in urban areas because the rooftops make the wind too turbulent. If you have a good, steady wind, put a turbine high on a pole away from your house.

- If a stream runs through your garden, a micro hydro system could provide you with a very steady electrical output. However, you need a good drop (a couple of metres is the absolute minimum) to get a decent output.

Discreet low-energy design. Look twice for the solar panels.

Chapter eight
Food security

The future of food

Food nourishes the home. For most of us, the kitchen and dining table are integral parts of our everyday lives and the complex process of sourcing foodstuffs, bringing them into the home, storing them, preparing them, consuming them and disposing of their waste is rich with meaning. If we are to prepare our homes and communities for the challenges of the century ahead, we must respect their dependence on, above all things, a secure supply of food.

A little global warming might be a good thing for food production in Britain. A rise in temperature of less than one degree has already extended the growing season, and new vineyards are being planted in the south of England in the expectation of an increasingly Mediterranean climate. There are even tea plantations in Cornwall. It is the view of the Intergovernmental Panel on Climate Change that 'moderate warming' of 1-3°C will have 'small beneficial impacts' on crop yields for high-latitude countries such as Britain.

Unfortunately, however, climate change is going to include much more than a little global warming. All the problems described in the earlier chapters in this book have profound consequences for food production. For example, in the European heatwave of 2003, French farmers saw their maize harvest reduced by 30 per cent and their fruit harvest reduced by 25 per cent.[1] Heatwaves also cause heat stress in livestock, reducing milk and meat production, and higher mean temperatures increase the range of pests and diseases. Prolonged drought can dramatically affect crop yields, as farmers in America, Australia and sub-Saharan Africa have all found to their cost in recent years. Floods and persistent rain can devastate agricultural land – during the very wet summer of 2007 Tesco resorted to sourcing its broccoli from the United States because European sources were under water.[2] Sea-level rise threatens fertile land through tidal floods, groundwater contamination and, ultimately, inundation.

Currently Britain's food security is underpinned by international trade. Half (51 per cent) of the food consumed in Britain is imported[3] and food retailers, especially supermarkets, are adept at delivering a consistent range of food in every season of the year. A food system with the capacity and flexibility to deliver strawberries in February is evidently well placed to maintain supplies of broccoli when the brassica fields of England are flooded. However, the complex supply infrastructure that supports this food system is itself vulnerable to weather shocks. The efficiency of the infrastructure under normal circumstances can make it vulnerable under abnormal circumstances;[4] low stocks and 'just in time' deliveries cannot be described as 'smart logistics solutions' when the roads are blocked by floods or storm damage. A day after the unexpected snowfall in the south-east of England in February 2009 the bread shelves of London supermarkets were empty.

Perhaps the food supply infrastructure can be adapted to become more resilient to weather shocks. No doubt the costs and benefits of doing so are already being considered by the multi-national organisations involved. However, there is a much more profound vulnerability within this system that will not be fixable in any straight-forward way: the dependence of every stage of the food chain on fossil fuels, from the manufacture of synthetic fertilisers to the heating of glasshouses full of unseasonal tomatoes and to the lorries, ships, aircraft and cars that bring the produce to our shops and homes. The modern, globalised food chain, perfected in the late twentieth century, is no longer fit for the twenty-first century, for it is a product of the era of cheap and plentiful fossil fuels and is almost unimaginable without them.

Chapter 7 identified the range of factors that threaten energy security in Britain, including declining national supplies of oil and gas, declining international supplies, political instability and climate change itself. Over and above these direct threats there is the global imperative to radically reduce greenhouse gas emissions and so reduce the risk of runaway climate change. The scale and complexity of these problems were made clear in 2008 when soaring oil prices pushed up the prices of basic food commodities across the world, triggering riots and pushing 40 million people into hunger.[5] The crisis was exacerbated by the transfer of millions of acres of arable land from food production to biofuels. If the modern food system is to overcome its dependence on oil, the change will have to be much more radical than such a simple switch of fuel source.

A year after the 2008 peak at $147 a barrel, the oil price had fallen back to double figures, the global economic downturn had reduced demand for oil and the price of commodities had fallen. This offered some reassurance to those who want to stick to the globalised food system to shore up our food security. Arguably, we may need to reduce the fossil-energy intensity of the system in the long run but there is no immediate crisis, and 2050 – the UK government's target date for reducing carbon emissions by 80 per cent – is still a long way off. Surely there is plenty of time for agribusiness to work out some smart solutions?

This argument is reasonable if the rest of the world is treated solely as a market that will, one way or another, continue to supply Britain's needs. But if we look beyond our own need for food security and consider the food security of human society as a whole, the challenge becomes much more acute and much more immediate. This is principally because the mean temperature rises that may have 'small beneficial effects' in northern latitudes will have immediately negative effects in southern latitudes. In countries where agriculture is already vulnerable to heat stress, an extra degree of warming and more frequent extreme events such as heatwaves and drought are potentially disastrous. These impacts are already being felt: climate change is already estimated to be causing 300,000 deaths worldwide per year, almost all of these in arid regions of the developing world.[6]

Many of the countries currently at risk from these climate change impacts have already suffered serious environmental impacts from soil degradation, pollution and water stress, undermining the capacity and resilience of their own agriculture. On top of this, population growth will dramatically increase demand for food in the next four decades – the Earth's population is projected to rise to 9.2 billion by 2050.[7] Like no other issue, food security exposes the interconnectedness of the problems of the modern world and the vulnerability of the societies in the front line of climate change.

If the food security of the North is sustained by a globalised, energy-intensive system that is already damaging the food security of the South, we need to start rethinking our food system straight away. The challenge is to radically reduce greenhouse gas emissions while also maintaining or improving food security. From a national perspective, this is a huge task. From a global perspective, taking account of increasing food shortages in heat-stressed nations, it is a monumental endeavour. It can, however, be done – and must be done, for everyone's sake, if runaway climate change is to be avoided.

The production, delivery, preparation, consumption and disposal of food accounts for 19 per cent of the UK's total greenhouse gas emissions.[8] The biggest source of emissions within the food chain is agriculture itself, which is dominated by nitrous oxide, released from fertilisers, and methane, emitted from both ends of cows and sheep (see Figure 8.1, overleaf). Although these two gases are released in smaller quantities than carbon dioxide, they have much more potent greenhouse effects. The principal sources of carbon dioxide in the food system are transport and food processing, both of which are highly energy-intensive. Unfortunately, every other stage of the food chain is also characterised by dependence on fossil fuels: at every turn we have opted for the high-energy solution. There are, therefore, a thousand opportunities to change our ways.

This chapter describes an approach to food production and consumption that reduces greenhouse gas emissions at almost every point along the food chain. At the same time, it shifts the focus of food supply from the international level to the regional, bringing food production closer to consumers and building stronger relationships between producers and consumers. Diversity of sourcing is maintained but the axis is local–regional rather than national–international.

It offers a vision of food security predicated not only on diversity of supply but also on the transformation of consumers from passive shoppers, blind to the distant powers that provide for them, to active participants in the food system.

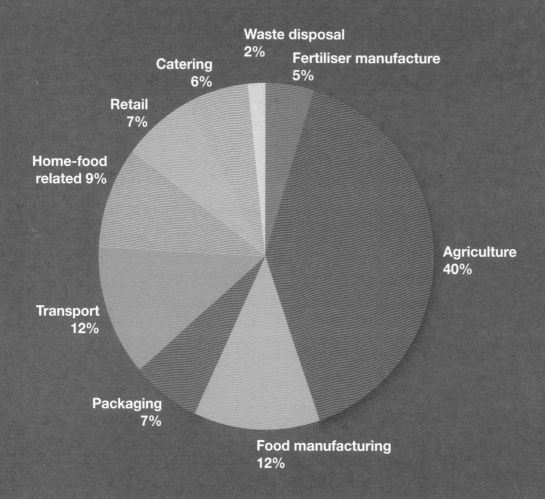

Figure 8.1. Greenhouse gas emissions linked to food consumed in the UK (estimates).[1]

	% UK GHG	% FOOD GHG
Fertiliser manufacture	0.9	5
Agriculture	7.6	40
Food manufacturing	2.3	12
Packaging	1.3	7
Transport	2.3	12
Home-food related	1.8	9
Retail	1.3	7
Catering	1.2	6
Waste disposal	0.3	2

An urban market garden, Hackney, London.

London, viewed from one of its many patches of determined digging.

Feeding the all-consuming metropolis: London

London is a world city: its population of seven million includes people from every nation on Earth. The needs, wants and consuming desires of this population are highly diverse and in the markets and shops of the city's hundred villages it seems that every food on Earth can be found. Draw a straight line across the map of London in any direction and you will slice through a cornucopia of international foodstuffs, such as *barfi* in the Indian sweet shops of Tooting, durians on the streets of Chinatown and *imam bayildi* in the Turkish restaurants of Haringay.

But there is local food in London too. In the window boxes, back gardens and allotments of the city, salad leaves, fruit and vegetables are tended and harvested throughout the year. The land available for food production within the city is small because the Victorian landowners who owned the patchwork of fields that once lay between the hundred villages were not slow to recognise the investment advantage of property over potatoes. Nonetheless, the guardians of the remaining fertile earth are passionate about its importance and the value of its produce to their health and quality of life.

London has never been self-sufficient in food, but for most of its history the infrastructure that supported the city was environmentally benign. This is perhaps what held the size of the city in check: when all London's food and fuel had to be brought in by horse and cart or sailboat, the population could not grow beyond a certain level without choking the slow supply lines. Few cities in the pre-industrial world grew beyond 100,000 people thanks to the simple logistics of daily food deliveries, though even in classical times durable goods such as grain were transported long distances by sea.[10] The arrival of fossil-fuel-driven trains, ships and motor vehicles overcame the constraints of the traditional food supply and allowed London to begin its extraordinary expansion. This ultimately enabled urban dwellers to become the majority of the world's population for the first time, in 2008.

In a single year, London consumes around seven million tonnes of food, 81 per cent of which is imported from outside the UK.[11] In comparison, the amount of food grown and consumed within the city itself is minuscule. However, this has not always been the case: in living memory there have been periods when London has produced a great deal of its own food. The 'Dig for Victory' campaign during the Second World War turned the royal parks into massive allotment sites and converted a million private rose gardens into vegetable patches. These physical measures, combined with rationing and a public expectation of a meagre diet, meant that Londoners got perhaps a quarter of the way to self-sufficiency. But most foodstuffs still had to be imported. Cities are viable only if they sustain productive relationships with the rural hinterland that provides for their needs.

The inner London borough of Hackney illustrates all the challenges of the modern food system: a population approaching a quarter of a million crammed into 19km², far from cultivated land and profoundly dependent for its daily bread on international markets and the complex supply infrastructure of the supermarkets. The level of poverty in the borough is high, so many residents rely on food prices staying low to get by.

Although Hackney has its fair share of social and economic problems, most local residents are proud of their area and happy to be there.[12] They are especially proud of their parks and open spaces – the borough has the best provision of green spaces in London, with 23 per cent of the land given over to parks and 19 per cent taken up with domestic gardens.[13] In such a densely populated area, these open spaces are vital to the health and well-being of the residents. For the most part, people go to the parks for fresh air, relaxation and exercise (Hackney Marshes is renowned for hosting the largest concentration of football

pitches in Europe). There are, however, a couple of corners where the land has been put to exceptionally productive use through the creation of miniature market gardens. These small parcels of land provide an unusually local, and therefore exceptionally fresh, supply of salad crops. Lettuces, tomatoes, basil and many other herbs are carefully tended by head gardener Ru Litherland, who brings further value to the sites by training local people as horticulture apprentices. After eight months of training, these apprentices then move on and, whenever possible, bring more of Hackney's land into cultivation. The long-term aim is to create a patchwork farm across the borough, myriad cooperative micro-sites hewn from large, underused back gardens, bits of public land and assorted neglected corners where other uses are not viable.

This patchwork inner-city farm is part of the vision of Growing Communities, a local community enterprise that aims to transform how people in urban settings understand and engage with the system that provides their daily nutrition. By cultivating land in the heart of Hackney, the organisation has a resource that is used not only to produce food for local people but also to educate and involve them in the experience of horticulture. This experience enables people to see food in a different light, no longer simply as a product on a supermarket shelf but as a precious resource, carefully tended and protected.

Changing attitudes is a first step, but Growing Communities' ambition is much greater than this. The organisation wants to create nothing less than a new food system that provides for the needs of local people without the environmental costs and consumer–producer dislocation that characterise the modern food industry. To achieve this, it must work not only with local residents in urban gardens but also with farmers in the broad rural hinterland, which has traditionally supplied the food needs of the capital. By building direct, supportive relationships from the heart of the all-consuming city, Growing Communities can free farmers from the constraints of the wholesale market and give them space to develop appropriate and sustainable methods of cultivation that will benefit producers and consumers alike.

Martin Mackie of Ripple Farm is one of the farmers participating in this 'Community Supported Agriculture' venture. Ripple Farm is also something of a patchwork – a collection of fields rented from various landowners in Kent, the county where Martin first trained in horticulture and has pursued independent farming ever since, though his origins are in Ireland. He knows what it is like to be an outsider in the farming business and how difficult it can be to plough your own furrow when the wholesale market and a few big buyers dominate the entire industry. Independent growers such as Martin cannot compete with the industrial farms that supply this market, so he too is keen to define and build an alternative system – a system that optimises environmental and human benefits rather than bottom-line profits. This is possible only by cutting out the wholesaler and building direct relationships with the consumer.

Friday is an important day for Martin and his small team as it is the day before the Stoke Newington Farmers' Market, the weekly market in north-west Hackney where all the farmers signed up by Growing Communities gather to sell their produce direct to local residents. The day starts early, harvesting rocket and lettuce for salad bags before moving half a mile down the road to gather aubergines and tomatoes from unheated green-houses, plus kale, calabrese and more salad from the surrounding fields. Then there is one more trip in the van to harvest carrots, cabbage, cauliflower and squash. All the harvesting is done by hand.

All Martin's land is certified organic so he uses no artificial fertilisers or pesticides. This means that considerable human effort is also expended on managing weeds. Many leaf crops are grown through weed-suppressant matting but the bigger crops such as brassicas are kept to the fore by uprooting the weeds early in the season using a simple 'earth-tickling' tool. Labour is not cheap, so it is easy to see how this approach to cultivation struggles to compete with pesticide-sprayed crops.

Across the Thames Estuary, in Essex, brothers Chris and Iain Learmouth are also preparing for the Stoke Newington Farmers' Market. Like Ripple Farm, Stocks Farm is viable only because of the active support of the people of Hackney. The farm developed bit by bit as the relationship with Growing Communities prospered. As a result, Chris and Iain also tend a scattered patchwork of rented fields, though recently they have been able to buy 30 acres of their own.

Stocks Farm is everything a typical industrial farm is not. It is small and piecemeal and the brothers cultivate and rear a wide variety of produce rather than just one or two crops. They try things out and see how they get on. As well as bringing an old

Salad crops are tended by head gardener Ru Litherland in one of Growing Communities' urban gardens.

orchard back into cultivation they have recently planted a new orchard, bringing to life one of Britain's thousands of neglected apple varieties, the Court Pendu Plat. They keep livestock – chickens, pigs, sheep and a cow or two – but only the pigs demand feed from beyond the productive land of the farm. As with all Growing Communities' suppliers, Chris and Iain's land is certified organic. Although this means that the output of the farm is lower than it would otherwise be, there are advantages to managing the land this way, for the growers as well as for the consumer: they do not need to bring bees on to the farm to pollinate the orchards, they do not have to prune the trees so hard, and they do not have to spend time and money spraying chemicals on their crops.

Market day in Hackney starts early, the stalls heaped high with produce only just out of the ground. Business is brisk and by the early afternoon the stalls start to look decidedly bare. Despite the economic downturn the market's trade has kept up, for the prices here reflect the genuine costs of production rather than the optimal supermarket profit. Although these costs are undoubtedly higher for independent growers, the direct relationship with the consumer helps to keep prices down. Unlike many farmers' markets, which are supplied from distant bulk growers and staffed by people who know nothing about the produce, all the stallholders in Stoke Newington know the provenance of their wares extremely well.

Beyond the farmers' market, Growing Communities also runs a successful box scheme. Boxes of seasonal produce are packed by a local team in Hackney and delivered to hundreds of households every week. Three-quarters of the produce that goes into the boxes is supplied by the city market gardens and the farmers of the region (in sharp contrast, less than 10 per cent of the fruit and vegetables consumed in Britain as a whole is grown within its borders[14]). Gaps in supply are filled from the organic wholesale market, which includes fruit from Europe when necessary.

Growing Communities may not be a big player in the multi-billion-pound retail food market

Martin Mackie and friends harvest vegetables at Ripple Farm in Kent.

in Britain, but nor is it simply a niche supplier. By making links between the locality and the region and between the consumer and the producer, the organisation has begun building its vision of an alternative food system. Food security within this system is still underpinned by a diversity of sources, but this diversity is predominantly regional rather than multinational. In the organisation's own analysis of how London's food needs could be met sustainably, 7.5 per cent of food would be grown within the city, 17.5 per cent on the city fringes (peri-urban), 35 per cent in the rural hinterland within 100 miles of the city, and 20 per cent in the rest of the UK. Twenty per cent would be imported, mostly from Europe.[15]

The relationships between consumers and producers and the greater awareness of consumers about the origins of their food are also important, for consumers who understand the problems that farmers are facing are much more likely to be flexible in their demands. Just as people will live with greater seasonality in their food choices once they understand the constraints of the seasons on their food supplies, so, as the effects of climate change start to be felt, perhaps they will come to appreciate the vulnerability of different crops to extreme weather events.

Community Supported Agriculture in the Growing Communities mould also significantly reduces the greenhouse gas emissions of the food supply chain. There are no energy-intensive fertilisers. On the farm, there is a minimum of mechanisation and artificial heating (only the baby chicks at Stocks Farm have a heater). Packaging is reduced

Ian and Chris Learmouth produce a wide range of organic produce on a scattering of plots in Essex.

to a few plastic bags for the salad leaves. The only transport used, other than on the farm itself, is from the farm to the market and from the box depot to individual homes. There are no retail sheds to light and heat. Food processing is minimal.

Only one big greenhouse gas problem remains: the 40 per cent of emissions resulting from agriculture itself (see Figure 8.1, page 150). The sheep and cows on Stocks Farm produce no less methane than the livestock on an ordinary farm, and organic manures are just as potent a source of nitrous oxide as artificial fertilisers. If greenhouse gases in the food system are divided across produce types rather than stages of the supply chain, meat and dairy products account for half of them.[16] Radical reductions in emissions from within the food chain will require that we look beyond the issue of how we produce food to the thornier issue of what we actually eat.

The edible city

Community Supported Agriculture will only ever be part of the solution. Nevertheless, projects such as Growing Communities demonstrate that there are real alternatives to the status quo – alternatives that benefit both producers and consumers while also helping to reduce the risks to more vulnerable communities in the global South. It may be hard to imagine the approach of Growing Communities scaled up to city level, but it is not impossible. Our dependence on the finely tuned, just-in-time, vertically integrated food system controlled by the supermarkets is profound, but this system is not the only way.

We might imagine the squares and streets of London regularly filled with markets supplied directly from the growers and producers in the rural hinterland; markets that attract all sections of the population with healthy, affordable produce. Such markets are still common in France, where the industrialisation of food has not completely wiped out traditional modes of producing and selling. We might even imagine the supermarkets rethinking their entire approach to supply-chain management, reshaping the wholesale market to prioritise local/regional, environmentally benign, seasonal supplies.

It is certainly possible to imagine thousands of people working on the land in and around London, supported by cooperatives that provide for their needs for seed and soil while also enabling the sale of produce through markets or local shops. This is the model that has been so successful in

Growing Communities' Sunday morning farmers' market in Stoke Newington, Hackney.

Cuba: the organic urban gardens or *organoponicos* of Havana have thrived not just because they meet a real need but also because there is a local infrastructure in place to support growers and consumers alike. There is such an infrastructure in London, but it is all but invisible to the ordinary consumer: an informal network of seed and plant swappers, manure shifters and cooperative fruit and vegetable sellers. It is a tiny part of the food culture of London but a joy to those who participate in it.

Happily, however, the idea of growing food in the city is no longer marginal. In London, waiting lists for allotments are heavily oversubscribed, so horticulture enthusiasts are looking beyond the established corners of vegetable growing to bring more of the city's land into productive use. The Capital Growth project is leading the way, aiming to create 2,012 new spaces for community food growing in the city by 2012. Given that food can be grown just about anywhere if you choose the right crop and put enough time and effort into improving the soil, this goal could be merely the starting point for a much wider transformation of food-growing in the metropolis.

There are neglected patches of land everywhere, if you look for them. On the Blenheim Gardens estate in Brixton, South London, local resident Bonnie Hewson is leading a campaign to turn the forgotten corners of the estate into productive land. The low-rise estate, built in the 1970s, is densely populated with compact terraces of two-storey houses and flats over garages. Most of the houses have small front and back yards, many of which are planted with shrubs. Bonnie, however, has her sights on the considerable areas of shared public space, much of which is underutilised.

In the turns and notches of the buildings and in the untrodden margins of public passageways, new raised beds have appeared, planted with salad leaves, herbs, brassicas and beans. Above the concrete bunkers where the estate's waste is stowed, forgotten roof gardens are being renewed; the compacted earth broken up and prepared for a return to cultivation. Compost is dug in before

potatoes are planted, a good crop for tough soil. A children's garden in the centre of the estate produces radishes, carrots, fennel and rainbow chard. As the visible evidence grows before them, more and more local people are seeing the value and rewards of living on an edible estate.

Bonnie leads a food group in the local Transition group,[17] Transition Town Brixton, which brings together similar enthusiasts from across the area. Little by little, neglected gardens, front yards, balconies and estates are being brought to productive life. It is early days but the great strength of the Transition movement is to see beyond the apparent certainties of the modern world, all of which (supermarkets included) are underpinned by a fragile dependence on fossil fuels, and imagine a different world that is sustainable, resilient and fair.[18]

The rural idyll

The scale of the challenge of urban food security provokes a question: why are we so devoted to living in cities in the first place? If cheap oil has made mega-cities viable, perhaps we should be rethinking our dependence on cities and making more productive, sustainable use of the broad countryside that feeds the city.

In Britain, thousands of people are keen to pursue such a rethink, dreaming the age-old dream of escaping the mayhem of urban life to a small plot of land where food can be produced all year round, life lived more slowly and something approaching self-sufficiency gained. There are thousands of smallholders and crofters in Britain already pursuing this dream, but there could be many more if planning regulations enabled agricultural land to be turned into horticultural homes – small but productive living environments where food was produced not for the distant masses but for the immediate needs of those who tended it.

Somewhere in the Forest of Dean in the west of England, Janine Michael and Andy Moore are

Bonnie Hewson and friends endeavour to create an edible estate in South London.

The rural idyll in the Forest of Dean. Theo tends the chickens, Andy makes the perry, Milo looks after the lambs and Janine harvests the vegetables.

pursuing this ideal on a modest two acres. Their bright whitewashed cottage sits at the bottom of a verdant gulley, framed by two ancient pear trees that provide an annual supply of sparkling perry. A south-facing embankment provides a perfect setting for a sprawling vegetable garden, with fruit bushes on the steeper ground. Chickens rescued from a battery farm potter about their generous pen, dazed by their new-found freedom. Further up the gulley, the two boys of the household, Milo and Theo, attend to a small flock of lambs. There are even trout in the brook that winds its way through the contours of the property. It is England's green and pleasant land in miniature.

In the modern world, however, this English rural idyll is inevitably not quite what it seems. To the south of the smallholding, a plastics factory raises its steel-tangled head above the treeline. To the north, a council estate spills down the hill. Janine and Andy have careers to pursue as well as vegetables to grow. Although both try to work from home as much as they can, two cars sit in the driveway. Their home is a delight, a tiny bucolic paradise, but it is not the beginning and end of their lives. They do not want to shut the gate and turn their backs on the world.

The old dream of self-sufficiency is still potent but the challenge today is not to return to a way of life that few of us could sustain in practice, however beguiling the idea might seem on a warm summer's day. Rather, the challenge is bring the key elements of the dream – the contact with the land, the joy of cultivation, the delight in home-grown food – into every corner of the modern world, exploiting opportunities whenever they arise.

What you can do

The issues raised by the modern food system are notoriously complex and the task of making the food supply chain genuinely sustainable is beset with traps and unintended consequences. For example, although transport is an obvious oil-burning source of carbon dioxide, a tomato grown in a heated greenhouse in Britain may have a higher carbon footprint than a tomato grown under the sun in Spain and trucked across the continent to a British supermarket. Similarly, an apple grown in Kent and kept in cold storage until the following summer may have a higher carbon footprint than an apple harvested in South Africa and shipped north for immediate consumption.[19] Nonetheless, there is a range of basic tenets which, taken together, point towards a more resilient, more sustainable and more equitable food chain.

- Grow your own. If you have only a window ledge, grow cut-and-come-again salad leaves, rocket and herbs. If you have a balcony, add tomatoes, beans, courgettes and a fruit tree against the wall (if it gets the sun). If you have a yard, garden or allotment, grow whatever thrives. If there is neglected ground in your estate, school, neighbourhood or churchyard, consider setting up a community garden.

- Minimise your consumption of meat and dairy products – treat meat as 'feast day food'. The meat and dairy industry is trying to reduce its emissions through improving feedstuffs and energy efficiency, but there is no escaping the size of the greenhouse gas burden of livestock farming. Although the world wants to eat more of these products, somehow we must learn to eat less.

- Wherever possible buy from, and get to know, the producer, especially producers from your region. This is straightforward only if you live near a farm shop or a genuine farmers' market. Alternatively, buy through intermediaries, such as box schemes, which keep you informed about the producers and the problems they face. Find out if there is a Community Supported Agriculture project in your area.

- Maximise your consumption of seasonal fruit and vegetables. A perishable crop eaten out of season will have been grown in an energy-intensive glasshouse, stored in an energy-intensive refrigerator or shipped from a foreign field.

- If local/regional supplies of your preferred food are interrupted because of extreme weather conditions, eat something else. As with seasonal produce, do not assume that everything will always be available.

- Minimise your consumption of imported food. This can be difficult in Britain because our domestic supply of fruit and vegetables is so small – but this is all the more reason to grow your own and seek out local/regional producers.

- Maximise your consumption of organic food, especially fruit, vegetables and cereals. Organic farmers focus on building soil fertility and maintaining the soil's natural ecosystem, trapping carbon and ensuring the long-term productivity of the land. Manures and legumes are used to enrich the soil rather than using artificial fertilisers, which are energy-intensive to produce.

- Minimise your consumption of processed foods. Modern processed foods are often highly energy-intensive to produce and are getting more so.

Food production is possible in every corner of the city, from neglected waste ground, transformed into allotments (left), to tower-block balconies (right).

Chapter nine
Future-proofing

Ahead of its time

The first British dwelling designed explicitly to cope with the impacts of climate change was built in 1997 in a quiet corner of Suffolk. Star Yard is the work of architect Neil Winder, whose interest in 'future-proofing' buildings for climate change is still a rare concern among his professional peers over a decade later.

Star Yard may have been groundbreaking but it does not appear so, at least not at first sight. It is certainly not out of place in the country lanes of East Anglia, where its simple form is like so many squarely built houses and cottages in the area and its timber weatherboarding is a familiar finish for houses, barns and agricultural sheds. It may not be a big house but it is attractive and generous, the exposed beams of the timber-frame construction

bringing warmth to the open-plan living room downstairs and to the three bedrooms upstairs. Jo, the current owner, loves the house and makes the most of the idyllic setting, tending roses and vegetables alike while chickens and cats vie for her attention.

The discreet details that together future-proof the building are by turns familiar, radical and down-right quirky. They start at the front door, which is all but hidden behind a cascade of vegetation that sprawls over the deep veranda shading the French windows on the south-facing ground floor. This principal line of defence against overheating is backed up by cross-ventilation: windows and doors can be opened at both ends of the open-plan living room to encourage breezes to blow through on summer days. Trees planted to the south-west have now grown high enough to shade the

Star Yard in Suffolk, designed by Neil Winder of architects Studio MGM.

building, as well as provide shelter from the prevailing wind.

The approach to the front door is along a raised wooden walkway that gives a clue to a more unusual feature of the building, namely that the entire structure is raised above the ground on concrete pads. Even in the heaviest rains, this house will never be at risk from surface flooding. The design also serves to minimise the risk of structural problems from ground movement if dry summers and wet winters become the norm. A flexible timber structure on these point foundations should cope well with repeated contraction and heave in the ground.

The strong, storm-resistant roof has big box gutters to cope with intense rainfall. As there is no mains drainage on the site, the gutters end in spouts that shed the rainwater away from the house into drainage ditches and, in passing, a water butt. This water butt is the only rainwater collector on site but the interior of the house is water-efficient, not least thanks to the composting toilet, which empties into simple chambers beneath the house.

If energy as well as water runs short, Jo will at least be able to stay warm in winter. The house is very well insulated and quickly warms up when one of the two wood-burning stoves is lit. The wood is coppiced from a small stand of willow trees planted in the back garden, then left to dry out in the adjacent barn. Electricity, however, is mains only and cooking relies on bottled liquid petroleum gas.

Star Yard demonstrates that building with the climate in mind need not to be onerous. Many of the details are unusual, which makes them unattractive to the risk-averse building profession, but they are not unaffordable. The issue is simply one of priorities – if the threat of climate change is taken seriously from the beginning of the design process, the design may follow unexpected paths, but there is no reason why the outcome should not be as attractive and liveable-in as any other. But will Star Yard cope well with climate change?

Only time will tell. Its weakness may prove to be its reliance on a northern European approach to passive cooling. The method adopted is to shade the main windows as best as possible, then use ventilation to clear any heat that builds up inside. But there is no external shading for the south-facing bedroom windows at the top of the house and cross-ventilation will be of little value when the outside air temperature is itself uncomfortably hot. What is missing is a cool refuge, an interior that is able to hold on to the cool of the night and can be completely protected from the heat of the day. The architect designed a lightweight building because he believed that the predicted rise in night-time temperatures would make it difficult for heavyweight buildings to cool down at night. But if the sun can be kept off key rooms throughout the day, it is possible to prevent a building heating up in the first place. The southern European idea of preserving the cool interior is still a foreign concept in temperate Britain.

For all its special characteristics, the most striking feature of Star Yard is its simplicity. In this, its similarity to old vernacular houses in the area is perhaps no coincidence. When houses are built with robustness and durability in mind, they tend to be simple and strong rather than complex and vulnerable. People have always gone back to basics when coping with extremes. With this simplicity comes a certain beauty that sits well with the semi-rural setting and is reflected in the pleasure Jo finds in the landscape, the garden and the chickens, and in a house with a radical agenda hidden by comfort and grace.

Away from it all

If simplicity offers a good starting point for climate-adaptive design, inspiration is perhaps best sought in those far-flung places to which people flee from the tumult of the modern world. One such place is the far north coast of Scotland, the flow country, where single-track roads wind their slow way round deep lochs in the shadow of ancient mountains. In the midst of this sparse, elemental landscape, Danish sculptor Lotte Glob

Top left: The shelter belt has matured to reach the upper bedroom windows.

Top centre: The entire building sits on concrete pads, raised off the ground.

Top right & bottom: A wood-burning stove is supplied by wood coppiced from a stand of sweet chestnut in the back garden.

Right: Large storm gutters shed rainwater away from the building into ditches.

has made her home in a house of beguilingly simple design. Its strong, unfussy lines provide a perfect frame for a spectacular view of water, rock and sky.

The house was designed by Gokay Devici for the existing climate of northern Scotland, not for a future climate, but the combination of low-cost, simple design with highly robust detailing makes it a shining example of a durable, climate-adaptive building. As with the houses by Dualchas Building Design described in Chapter 6, storms and gales are the first concern, so the building form is highly aerodynamic with minimal protrusions and an exceptionally strong roof. In this case, however, the wind can get under the building as it sits on stilts above the boggy moor. This feature makes the house flood-resistant but means that the structure has to be tied together very securely to prevent the entire building taking off.

The big picture window that dominates the house is protected from the rain by a large canopy – a feature that also protects the glazing and the room inside from the high summer sun. Like Star Yard, this is a lightweight building, but the overheating risk in this location is likely to remain low for a long time to come, so shading should be enough to keep it to a minimum. Coping with the cold will probably remain the priority, so the house is super-insulated and has a wood-burning stove that provides heat in the winter.

The Lotte Glob House represents an idyll that many people who worry about the impacts of climate change hanker after: far away from the chaos of the city; simple and beautiful; robust on its hill above a relatively unthreatened coast. For most of us, however, this idyll will remain an impractical dream. The challenge, therefore, is to see how the ideas of robust design can be applied just as successfully in communities and cities.

The autonomous community

If you were to design and build a small community housing development from scratch in a manner that addressed every one of the issues considered in this book, you would be hard pushed to improve upon the design of the Hockerton Housing Project. This is despite the fact that long-term resilience to the effects of climate change was not a design consideration, let alone a priority, for architects Robert and Brenda Vale.

Left: The Lotte Glob House: a simple, low-cost, robust design.
Right: The highly insulated building is heated by a wood-burning stove when necessary.

The Hockerton Housing Project, an autonomous community in Nottinghamshire.

For them, and their client, the agenda was all about reducing environmental impacts and maximising ecological sustainability. Built in the 1990s, Hockerton Housing is a famous British exemplar of community eco-housing.

The project consists of five homes and a business built, unusually, on what was previously agricultural land on the edge of the small village of Hockerton in Nottinghamshire. One reason that planning permission for the change of use was gained was that the local authority was persuaded that the project was going to be something quite different from the usual dormitory development for commuters. The inclusion of the business on site was crucial to making this case, but the ambition of the project developers was much greater than this – they wanted to create a

community that was, as far as possible, self-sufficient. Impressed by the Vales' earlier 'autonomous house',[1] they wanted to pursue the idea of autonomy further – imagining, designing and building something that comes quite close to being a genuinely autonomous community.

Approaching the development from the back, it is easy to fail to see it until you are almost upon it, for all five single-storey houses are earth-bermed, hidden from the north beneath a great cowl of earth, grass, nettles and flowers. Although the winds of the Western Isles are rarely experienced in rural Nottinghamshire, this long, low, landscape-integrated form is highly evocative of the black houses and their supremely wind-shedding design, described in Chapter 6. Combined with a shelter belt of trees

The low, earth-bermed design is highly storm-resistant.

to the south-west (the direction of the prevailing wind), the development is likely to cope well with the fiercest of future gales.

The form of the development is driven by the priorities of 'passive solar' design. In order to minimise energy needs, the heavyweight concrete houses face directly south through a glass facade that runs the length of the terrace. The heavy materials, surrounded by thick insulation, absorb the heat of the low autumn and winter sun, minimising the need for active heating. The heat of the sun, the occupants and their cooking is just enough to keep the homes at a comfortable temperature in the winter. There is no central heating. The energy needed for lights, cooking and appliances is generated by two wind turbines and a long strip of photovoltaic panels just below the

flowering ridge of the terrace. As on Eigg, the design combines renewable technologies in such a way that power is generated whatever the weather. When the sun shines, the photovoltaic panels kick in; when the wind blows, the turbines take over. Unlike Eigg, however, the project is connected to the national grid and so does not have to rely on batteries and generators for back-up. Battery back-up has long been planned; it is, after all, one step closer to the autonomous ideal.

But surely that expanse of south-facing glass means that the houses will be increasingly at risk from overheating? Passive solar energy may be great in the chill of winter but it is far from welcome in a summer heatwave. Without doubt this is a risk of passive solar design, yet Hockerton escapes this outcome, in part because of the great

Top: All electricity needs at Hockerton are provided by wind turbines and solar panels.

Bottom: The conservatories trap heat when it is needed in winter but the cool interiors beyond them are protected in the heat of the summer.

Left: A reservoir, filled with rainwater, supplies all water except drinking water.
Right: Drinking water is collected on the roofs and stored underground.

cooling green roof above and, more importantly, because of the subtlety with which solar heat is controlled within the buildings.

The broad glass frontage of the terrace does not open directly on to the main living space but on to a deep conservatory that sits outside the insulated envelope of the building. In the winter, the low sun penetrates the conservatory and reaches through the windows and doors of the living spaces to the very back of the building. When the conservatory warms up, doors and windows are opened to allow the heat to flow into the interior spaces. In the summer, the high sun penetrates the conservatory roof but the main living space is shaded. Conservatory windows and roof vents are opened to flush the heat out but the doors and windows of the living spaces are closed to keep the heat beyond the insulated walls. Thus the concrete and tiles of the conservatory provide a heat store in winter and a cool store in summer. If the residents are as diligent as the people of Seville in protecting their cool interiors, they should be able to sleep comfortably even in the hottest of future summers.

Hot summers could also threaten the local water supply, for Hockerton Housing has no connection to mains water or sewerage services. Every drop of water consumed on site is rainwater, collected from the immediate environment. Fortunately, however, the catchment area for this water supply is substantial: ditches run across an eight-acre area, draining water from the surrounding land to an underground sump from where it is pumped to a reservoir at the high point of the land. From here it is put through a simple sand filter before being used in the homes for everything but drinking and cooking. The reservoir has a capacity of 150m³, enough to maintain a supply of non-potable water for a hundred days. Low-flush toilets, flow restrictors on showers and water-efficient appliances all help to minimise the consumption of the water and so reduce the demand on the reservoir.

As drinking water requires a much higher standard of purity an independent supply is maintained, sourced from the roofs only. As in the old houses of Santorini, described in Chapter 4, this rainwater is directed straight to underground chambers where it is protected from the bacterial

Half of the residents' food needs are grown or produced on site.

growth that sunlight stimulates. Even so, substantial filtration is needed, including a UV filter, to ensure the water is fit for drinking. The tanks can hold enough to keep the residents in drinking water for 250 days. Sewerage relies on separation tanks, which supply both the compost heap and a reed-bed system that eventually flows into the artificial lake in front of the development. The water in this lake has been regularly tested and consistently found to be of excellent quality.

Despite the close proximity of the houses to this lake, the threat from flooding is minimal. The only possible source of flooding is rainwater as there are no nearby rivers to make room for. As almost every surface within the bounds of the development is absorbent, including the walls and roofs of the houses, and as water that drains from the land is constantly moved up to the reservoir, there is little chance of surface water build-up.

This soft green landscape is used not only for collecting rainwater but also for food production. A substantial vegetable garden, with its own rainwater supply, is complemented by a small flock of sheep. The output from these two sources is enough to provide approximately half of the residents' food. More land could be brought into cultivation, but the residents all contribute to the management of the land in their spare time. None

wants to be a full-time smallholder. The substantial amount of food they do produce is therefore testament to the efficiency of their collective effort.

Without question, collective effort is needed to sustain the Hockerton Housing Project, and anyone moving in must agree to participate in the shared responsibilities of the project: maintaining the water filtration and sewerage systems, servicing the wind turbines, looking after the sheep, and even showing people round and educating groups about sustainable design. Not everyone wants this level of community participation and not everyone wants to live in a gentle rural paradise. Yet even in the anonymous city, the model is potent. However individualistic we want to be, we have to work together if we want to live sustainably and prepare for an uncertain future.

The soft and hairy city

In the heart of the well-to-do London suburb of Islington, the streets bake under the midsummer sun. The handsome terraces, built by speculative developers in the nineteenth and early twentieth century, are packed into the available space, with front doors only a few steps from the pavement edge. There are few front gardens, though some

The glorious green roofs of Justin Bere's home and architectural studio in Newington Green, London.

The primary garden is an English meadow, which requires minimal watering and attracts a multitude of native insects and birds.

Foxgloves for the delight of humans and the nourishment of bumblebees.

streets enjoy the shade of mature broadleaved trees. The landscape is defined by masonry, brick and tarmac.

The street frontages are ordered, elegant and, on the whole, well maintained. In contrast, the backs of the homes are a disorderly muddle of extensions, yards, sheds and the occasional micro-garden. The residents do their best to make the most of assorted awkward spaces: narrow side returns, tiny courtyards and unlikely balconies. In among them, shops, industrial units and motor workshops compete for space. Between the back yards of two parallel streets in Newington Green, a Turkish sausage factory once churned out its daily produce. But the factory has gone, its

scrubbed floors and stinking vents replaced by the striking home and studio of Justin Bere, an architect who has the imagination to conceive of the urban landscape as an extension, a reinter-pretation, of the natural landscape it replaces.

There are four distinct green roofs on Justin's home-cum-studio. Each is planted to a different depth and sustains a different micro-ecosystem. At the very top of the building, sharing space with a solar panel, the soil is thin and only the hardiest of drought-tolerant, creeping plants survive. One level down, the soil is deeper and an English meadow blooms with daisies, cornflowers, viper's bugloss and the aphid-friendly common vetch. At the other end of the building, hawthorn is underplanted with purple and white foxgloves and oxeye daisies. At the lowest level, where humans rather than insects gather, fuchsia flowers amid crocosmia. Only the latter two gardens need the occasional watering, supplied by a rainwater tank that takes the run-off from the gardens themselves. The gardens attract insects and the insects attract birds: wrens and house sparrows; blackbirds and great tits; goldfinches and starlings. Honeybees and bumble bees throng the bright summer flowers. The rear windows of the dozen houses surrounding the plot look down upon a tiny, urban Eden.

Delight and biodiversity may be the most obvious functions of these green roofs of Newington Green, but there are many more benefits for inhabitants, neighbours and wildlife alike. The plants clean and purify the polluted city air. The thick earth roof keeps the rooms below cool in the heat of summer. The asphalt roof protection below the earth is itself protected from UV radiation by the soil and so does not deteriorate and become vulnerable to storm damage. When heavy rains hit the roofs, the earth soaks up the rainwater, keeping the pressure off the overloaded drains and so reducing the risk of flash floods. The tank that takes up the rainwater is big enough to see the gardens, with their limited needs, through a prolonged drought. Almost everything we need to successfully adapt to the changing climate of the twenty-first century is here. There is even a beehive to support the urban food growers of inner London.

Imagine a city that is soft and hairy; green and blue; where vegetation and water define the form, character and details of the urban fabric. Imagine a city that is cooled by deep, luxuriant planting; a city that is permeable, absorbing and capturing rainwater to maintain ground conditions and sustain its flora and fauna (humans included); a city that makes space for water such that it can take up the floodwaters when the rains are relentless or the rivers overtop; a city where food grows on every corner and rooftop; a city so well adapted to seasonal temperature variations that minimal energy is needed to keep its citizens comfortable in their homes; a city where birdsong fills the air.

Is this Babylon in 600 BCE? Hampi in 1500 CE? Oz in 1939? Or London in 2050? We can be sure of only the last of these. Assuming, of course, that we set our hearts and minds to the task today.

The soft and hairy city, attractive to creatures of all sizes.

Afterword

With a few exceptions, architects, engineers and planners are yet to face up to the implications of climate change for the design of their twenty-first century buildings and neighbourhoods. It has been a big enough challenge rethinking how we build our homes and plan our communities to reduce our impact on the climate, let alone worrying about the long-term impacts of the climate on us. Yet the houses and cities we build today will still be standing, for the most part, when these impacts hit home. Arguably, some of these changes are with us already. Surely, then, it is vital that everyone involved in designing and building our collective future takes a broader view.

This book could, however, be criticised for taking too narrow a view. Although there has been a constant emphasis throughout on the need to link strategies for dwellings with strategies for neighbourhoods, regions and even nations, the focus has remained squarely on the built environment. The kinds of thresholds considered have been physical thresholds: the points at which our homes get too hot, or the water runs out, or the flood defences are overtopped. These thresholds are relatively easy to specify, even if we cannot be sure when they will be reached.

The chapters on energy security and food security began to point towards the wider issues of social vulnerability. These issues are far more complex than matters of building design because they concern how we cope as individuals, societies and a world community as the physical impacts get ever-more serious. They concern our values, our economies, our politics and our humanity, all of which will be challenged in the years ahead.[1] Although this book has not addressed these issues in any depth, it ends with an acknowledgement that our skills in building for the future will mean little if we do not have the imagination and vision to cooperate and tackle these wider problems together. Just as there are traditions of building for extremes from which to draw inspiration, so every society has a history of openness and generosity in the face of suffering, loss and hardship. If we revisit these histories and remember what we are capable of, we can face the future with hope and humility.

TO THE GLORY OF GOD & IN GRATEFUL MEMORY OF H. M. KING EDWARD VI WHO BY HIS CHARTER OF 1550 GRANTED ASYLUM TO THE HUGUENOTS FROM FRANCE THIS TYMPANUM WAS SET UP IN THE YEAR OF OUR LORD 1950

The tympanum of the French Protestant Church, Soho Square, London.

References

Introduction

1 Defra (Department for Environment, Food and Rural Affairs) (2009) *Adapting to Climate Change. UK Climate Projections.* June 2009.

2 Global Humanitarian Forum (2009). *The Anatomy of a Silent Crisis.*

Chapter one:
The future unfolds

1 For an overview, see Defra (2009) *Adapting to Climate Change. UK Climate Projections.* For a fuller account of the methods and findings, see Murphy, J. et al. (2009) *UK Climate Projections science report: Climate change projections*, Met Office Hadley Centre, Exeter. For details of sea-level changes, see Lowe, J. A. et al. (2009) *UK Climate Projections science report: Marine and coastal projections*, Met Office Hadley Centre, Exeter. Interactive maps can be accessed via the UK Climate Projections website http://ukclimateprojections.defra.gov.uk.

2 Defra (2009) *Adapting to Climate Change. UK Climate Projections.* June 2009.

Chapter two: Heatwaves

1 The Cabinet Office (2008) *National Risk Register.*

2 Wood, R. and Wallace, C. (2009) 'Changes to the Atlantic Ocean circulation (Gulf Stream)', in Murphy, J. et al. *UK Climate Projections science report: Climate change projections*. Met Office Hadley Centre, Exeter.

3 Watkins, R., Littlefair, P., Kolokotroni, M. and Palmer, J. (2002) 'The London heat island – surface and air temperatures in a park and gorges'. ASHRAE winter meeting 2002, Atlantic City. Summarised in Watkins, R., Palmer, J. and Kolokotroni, M. (2007) 'Increased temperature and intensification of the urban heat island: implications for human comfort and urban design'. *Built Environment* 33(1): 85-96.

4 Barrionuevo, A. and Torres, F. (1979) 'Séville et la maison sur cour'. *Werk/Archithese* 66: 49-54.

5 Hyde (ed.) (2008) *Bioclimatic Housing: Innovative designs for warmer climates.* Earthscan, London.

6 Wilby, R. L. (2003) 'Past and projected trends in London's urban heat island'. *Weather* 58: 251-60.

7 Watkins, R., Palmer, J. and Kolokotroni, M. (2007) 'Increased temperature and intensification of the urban heat island: implications for human comfort and urban design'. *Built Environment*, 33(1): 85-96.

8 Watkins, Palmer and Kolokotroni, ibid.

9 Imperial College (2003) 'Scientists formulate a heat wave survival guide'. Imperial College press release, 6 August 2003.

10 Chartered Institute of Building Service Engineers (2005) *Climate Change and the Indoor Environment: Impacts and adaptation.* CIBSE, London.

Chapter three: Floods

1 Pitt, M. (2007) *Learning the Lessons of the 2007 Floods* (The Pitt Review). The Cabinet Office.

2 Waterland Water Information Network, www.waterland.net.

3 Thorne, C. R., Evans, E. P. and Penning-Rowsell, E. C. (eds) (2007) *Future Flooding and Coastal Erosion Risks*. Thomas Telford Books, London.

4 Greater London Authority. (2002) *Crazy Paving: The environmental importance of London's front gardens*.

5 Department of Communities and Local Government (2006) *Planning Policy Statement 25: Development and Flood Risk*. HMSO.

Chapter four: Drought

1 Institute of Mechanical Engineers (2009) *Climate Change: Adapting to the inevitable?* IMechE, London.

2 Environment Agency (2008) *Climate Change and River Flows in the 2050s*. Science Summary SC070079/SS1.

3 Stasinopoulos, T. N. (2006) 'The four elements of Santorini architecture – lessons in vernacular sustainability'. 23rd International Conference on Passive and Low Energy Architecture, 6-8 Sept 2006, Geneva, Switzerland.

4 Avlonitis, S. A., Kouroumbas, K. and Vlachakis, N. (2003) 'Energy consumption and membrane replacement cost for seawater RO desalination plants'. *Desalination* 157: 151-8.

5 Pandey, D. N., Gupta, A. K. and Anderson, D. M. (2003) 'Rainwater harvesting as an adaptation to climate change'. *Current Science* 85(1): 46-59.

6 Agarwal, A. and Narain, S. (1992) 'Traditional systems of water harvesting and agroforestry', in Sen, G. *Indigenous Vision – People of India attitudes to the environment*. India International Centre, Sage Publications, New Delhi.

7 Defra (2008) *Future Water: The government's water strategy for England*.

8 For a full technical description of the options for grey water reuse, see Thornton, J. (2008) *The Water Book*. Centre for Alternative Technology, Machynlleth.

9 Hughes, R. (2007) 'Did the Earth move for you? Buying a house? Every house-buyer in the UK could benefit from a new geological hazard service from the British Geological Survey.' *Planet Earth*, Spring 2007, 24-5.

Chapter five: Threatened coasts

1 Meehl, G. A. et al. (2007): 'Global climate projections', in Solomon, S. et al. *Climate Change 2007: The Physical Science Basis. Contribution of Working Group I to the Fourth Assessment Report of the Intergovernmental Panel on Climate Change*. Cambridge University Press, Cambridge, UK and New York, USA.

2 Lowe, J. A. et al. (2009) *UK Climate Projections science report: Marine and coastal projections*. Met Office Hadley Centre, Exeter.

3 Rohling, E. J. et al (2008) 'High rates of sea level rise during the last interglacial period'. *Nature Geoscience* 1: 38-42.

4 Based on Table 3.3, Lowe et al., op. cit.

5 Lowe et al., op. cit.

6 The National Trust (2005) *Shifting Shores: Living with a changing coastline*.

7 Weston, C. and Weston, S. (1994) *Claimed by the Sea*. Wood Green Publications, Norwich.

8 Coastal Concern Action Group. Notes from three village meetings, 2008. www.happisburgh.org.uk.

9 Defra (2009) *Appraisal of Flood and Coastal Erosion Risk Management*. Defra policy statement, June 2009.

10 North Norfolk District Council (2007) *Kelling to Lowestoft Ness Shoreline Management Plan* (first review).

11 Stansby, P., Kuang, C.-P., Laurence. D. and Launder, B. (2006) *Sandbanks for Coastal Protection: Implications of sea-level rise. Part 1: Application to East Anglia.* Tyndall Centre for Climate Change Research, University of East Anglia, Norwich.

12 North Norfolk District Council (2004). *Kelling to Lowestoft Ness Shoreline Management Plan.*

13 Thorne, C. R., Evans, E. P. and Penning-Rowsell, E. C. (eds) (2007) *Future Flooding and Coastal Erosion Risks.* Thomas Telford Books, London.

14 Attributed to Rahm Emanuel, Barack Obama's chief of staff, reflecting on the global financial crisis of 2008-9.

15 An assessment of the impact of a five-metre sea-level rise concluded that the response in the Thames estuary would be 'a mix of protection, accommodation and retreat, with parts of the city centre turned into a Venice of London'. Tol, R. S. J. et al. (2006) 'Adaptation to five metres of sea level rise'. *Journal of Risk Research* 9: 467-82.

16 In June 2009, the mayor of London welcomed a new water infrastructure to service the 2012 London Olympic Games with the words: "The revitalisation of this network of canals after decades of decline heralds a new age of water transport in the capital."

Chapter six: Storms

1 Alexander, L. V., Tett, S. F. B. and Jonsson, T. (2005) 'Recent observed changes in severe storms over the United Kingdom and Iceland'. *Geophysical Research Letters* 32, L13704, doi:10.1029/2005GL022371.

2 For example: WWF (2006) *Stormy Europe – The power sector and extreme weather.*

3 Christensen, J. H. et al. (2007) 'Regional climate projections', in Solomon, S. et al. *Climate Change 2007: The Physical Science Basis. Contribution of Working Group I to the Fourth Assessment Report of the Intergovernmental Panel on Climate Change.* Cambridge University Press, Cambridge, UK and New York, USA.

4 Hulme, M. et al. (2002) *Climate Change Scenarios for the United Kingdom: The UKCIP02 Scientific Report.* Tyndall Centre for Climate Change Research, University of East Anglia, Norwich.

5 Brown, S. (2009) 'Annex 6: Future changes in storms and anticyclones affecting the UK', in Murphy, J. et al. *UK Climate Projections science report: Climate change projections.* Met Office Hadley Centre, Exeter.

6 Allan, R., Tett, S, and Alexander, L. (2009) 'Fluctuations in autumn–winter severe storms over the British Isles: 1920 to present'. *International Journal of Climatology* 29: 357-71.

7 Meehl, G. A. et al. (2007): 'Global climate projections', in Solomon, S. et al. *Climate Change 2007: The Physical Science Basis. Contribution of Working Group I to the Fourth Assessment Report of the Intergovernmental Panel on Climate Change.* Cambridge University Press, Cambridge, UK and New York, USA.

8 Dlugolecki, A. (2004) *A Changing Climate for Insurance – Technical Annex.* Association of British Insurers, London.

9 Roaf, S., Crichton, D. and Nicol, F. (2005) *Adapting Buildings and Cities for Climate Change.* Architectural Press, Oxford.

10 Murphy, J. et al. (2009) *UK Climate Projections science report: Climate change projections.* Met Office Hadley Centre, Exeter.

11 Graves, H. M. and Phillipson, M. C. (2000) *Potential Implications of Climate Change in the Built Environment.* Foundation for the Built Environment Report 2, BRE, Watford.

12 Walker, B. (1989) 'Edited notes on Hebridean Buildings from Ake Campbell's field notebooks of July 1948'. *Vernacular Building* (Scottish Vernacular Buildings Working Group), 13: 47-65.

13 For a full account of the decline and fall of the black houses of Lewis, see Mackie, C. (2006) 'The development of traditional housing in the Isle of Lewis: social and cultural influences on vernacular architecture'. *Béaloideas* 74: 65-102.

14 Building Research Establishment (BRE) (1995) 'Wind actions on buildings and structures'. *BRE Digest* no. 406, June 1995.

Chapter seven: Energy security

1 50,000 homes in Leicestershire (not a county renowned for severe weather) were left without power in 2006 following severe storms. BBC News Online, 6 July 2006.

2 DTI (Department of Trade and Industry) (2007) *Meeting the Energy Challenge*. A White Paper on Energy, May 2007.

3 Organisation of Petroleum Exporting Countries (OPEC) (2008) *World Oil Outlook 2008*.

4 See Campbell, C. J. (2005) *Oil Crisis*, Multi-Science Publishing Company, or the many resources available through the website of the Association for the Study of Peak Oil and Gas (www.peakoil.net).

5 International Energy Agency. *World Energy Outlook 2008*.

6 Monbiot, G. (2008) 'When will the oil run out?' *The Guardian*, 15 December 2008.

7 Pagnamenta, R. (2008) 'National Grid chief Steve Holliday: blackouts will be common in 7 years'. *The Times*, 22 December 2008.

8 Defra, BERR (Department for Business, Enterprise and Regulatory Reform) (2008) *The UK Fuel Poverty Strategy, 6th Annual Progress Report*.

9 Rosen, N. (2007) *How to Live Off-Grid: Journeys outside the system*. Doubleday, London.

10 See www.thatroundhouse.info.

11 Centre for Alternative Technology (2007) *Zero Carbon Britain: An alternative energy strategy*. CAT, Machynlleth.

12 DECC (Department for Energy and Climate Change) (2008) *Digest of UK Energy Statistics 2008*.

Chapter eight: Food security

1 Easterling, W. E., Aggarwal, P. K. et al. (2007) 'Food, fibre and forest products' in *Climate Change 2007: Impacts, Adaptation and Vulnerability. Contribution of Working Group II to the Fourth Assessment Report of the Intergovernmental Panel on Climate Change*. Cambridge University Press.

2 Garnett, T. (2008) *Cooking Up a Storm: Food, greenhouse gas emissions and our changing climate*. Food Climate Research Network, Centre for Environmental Strategy, University of Surrey.

3 Defra (2008) *Food Statistics Pocketbook 2008*.

4 Defra (2006) *Food Security and the UK: An evidence and analysis paper*.

5 Food and Agriculture Organization of the United Nations (2008) 'Number of hungry people rises to 963 million'. Press release, 9 December 2008.

6 Global Humanitarian Forum (2009) *The Anatomy of a Silent Crisis*.

7 Population Division of the Department of Economic and Social Affairs of the United Nations Secretariat (2008) *World Population Prospects: The 2007 revision*.

8 Garnett, T. op. cit.

9 Garnett, T. op. cit. Figure 4: Food and its contribution to GHG emissions – a consumption-oriented perspective.

10 Steel, C. (2008) *Hungry City. How food shapes our lives*. Vintage, London.

11 Best Foot Forward (2002) *City Limits: A resource flow and ecological footprint analysis of Greater London.* Chartered Institution of Wastes Management Environmental Body.

12 Ipsos MORI (2007) *Best Value General User Survey 2006-07.* Research study conducted for London Borough of Hackney.

13 Office for National Statistics (2008) *Neighbourhood Statistics.*

14 Defra (2008) *Food Statistics Pocketbook 2008.*

15 Kerry Rankine, Growing Communities, Pers. comm. 3 April 2009. With reference to Growing Communities' food zones diagram. (See Pinkerton, T. (2009) *Local Food.* Green Books, Dartington.)

16 Kramer, K. J., Moll, H. C., Nonhebel, S. and Wilting, H. C. (2008) 'Greenhouse gas emissions related to Dutch food consumption'. *Energy Policy* 27: 203-21.

17 The Transition movement is a global network of local initiatives to raise awareness of and respond to the challenges of peak oil and climate change.

18 See Hopkins, R. (2008) *The Transition Handbook: From oil dependency to local resilience.* Green Books, Dartington.

19 Milà i Canals, L., Cowell, S. J., Sim, S. and Basson, L. (2007) 'Comparing domestic versus imported apples: a focus on energy use'. *Environmental Science Pollution Research International* 14(5): 338-44.

Chapter nine: Future-proofing

1 Vale, B. and Vale, R. (2000) *The new Autonomous House.* Thames & Hudson, London.

Afterword

1 For a well-grounded analysis of five possible world futures in response to climate change, see Forum for the Future (2008) *Climate Futures: Responses to climate change in 2030.*

Resources

Act on CO$_2$
http://actonco2.direct.gov.uk
Government campaign providing advice and information on reducing individual and household carbon emissions.

AECB The Sustainable Building Association
www.aecb.net, 0845 456 9773
A network of individuals and companies promoting best practice in environmentally sustainable building.

BigBarn
www.bigbarn.co.uk, 01480 890970
Directory of local food in the UK.

Capital Growth
www.capitalgrowth.org, 020 7837 1228
Project aiming to create 2,012 new community food-growing spaces in London by 2012.

Centre for Alternative Technology
www.cat.org.uk, 01654 705950
Information, publications and training on renewable energy technology and ecological building.

Certified Farmers' Markets
www.farmersmarkets.net, 0845 458 8420
Directory of UK farmers' markets certified by the National Farmers' Retail and Markets Association.

Department for Environment, Food and Rural Affairs
www.defra.gov.uk, 0845 933 5577
Government department with responsibility for climate change adaptation.

Energy Saving Trust
www.energysavingtrust.org.uk, 0800 512012
Provides extensive advice and information on domestic energy-efficiency improvements and renewable energy systems, including information on local grants.

Environment Agency
www.environment-agency.gov.uk, 0870 850 6506
Key government agency with responsibility for managing risks of river flooding, coastal erosion and drought in England and Wales. Local flood-risk maps and current flood warnings are available through the website. Provides information for householders on reducing flood risks, improving water efficiency and responding to coastal erosion.

Flood Protection Association
www.floodprotectionassoc.co.uk, 0844 335 8457
Trade association with company contacts and case studies.

Flood Resilient Project
www.floodresilienthome.com
Produced by the insurance company AVIVA, the website offers advice and information on improving the flood resilience of your home.

Floodline
0845 988 1188
Current flood warnings and advice, provided by the Environment Agency and Scottish Environment Protection Agency

Green Building Press
www.newbuilder.co.uk
Publications and online forums addressing all aspects of ecological building.

Intergovernmental Panel on Climate Change
www.ipcc.ch
The world's leading authority on climate change. The IPCC's regular publications include reports on the impacts of climate change.

Living Roofs
www.livingroofs.org
Promotes green roofs of all kinds on all types of property.

Low Carbon Buildings Programme
www.lowcarbonbuildings.org.uk, 0800 915 0990
Grants for the installation of renewable microtechnology such as solar panels and wind turbines.

Making Local Food Work
www.makinglocalfoodwork.co.uk, 01993 810730
Supports the development of the many links in a more localised food chain.

Met Office
www.metoffice.gov.uk, 0870 900 0100
Vital source of information on the weather, the climate and climate change in the UK. Hosts the Hadley Centre, the UK's leading climate-change research centre.

National Flood Forum
www.floodforum.org.uk, 01299 403055
An independent source of advice and information for those who are at risk of flooding or have been affected by flooding. Publishes a guide to the products available in the UK to improve flood resilience.

National Voice of Coastal Communities
www.nvcc.org.uk
Campaigns for social justice for coastal communities affected by erosion.

Northern Ireland Environment Agency
www.ni-environment.gov.uk, 0845 302 0008
The government agency in Northern Ireland responsible for climate change and water-resource issues.

Northern Ireland Rivers Agency
www.riversagencyni.gov.uk, 02890 253355
The government agency in Northern Ireland responsible for rivers and flood defences. The flood emergency telephone helpline for Northern Ireland is 0300 2000 100.

Scottish Environmental Protection Agency
www.sepa.org.uk, 01786 457700
The government agency in Scotland responsible for climate change, flooding and wider water-resource issues.

Sustainable Energy Academy
www.sustainable-energyacademy.org.uk, 01908 665555
Information and case studies illustrating radical improvements in the energy performance of existing homes.

Town and Country Planning Association
www.tcpa.org.uk, 020 7930 8903
Think tank that has highlighted the wide range of interventions needed to adapt to climate change in the UK.

Tyndall Centre for Climate Change Research
www.tyndall.ac.uk, 01603 593900
Leading UK academic centre with a programme of multidisciplinary research into climate-change adaptation.

UK Climate Impacts Programme
www.ukcip.org.uk, 01865 285717
Coordinates the production and dissemination of the UK's climate projections and promotes adaptive responses to climate change.

The UK Rainwater Harvesting Association
www.ukrha.org
Trade association providing information and company contacts.

Waterwise
www.waterwise.org.uk, 020 7344 1882
Independent advice and information on all aspects of water efficiency.

Index

Page numbers in italic refer to figures and illustrations. Those in bold refer to whole chapters.